#tweetsmart

J.S. McDougall

O'REILLY®

Beijing · Cambridge · Farnham · Köln · Sebastopol · Tokyo

#tweetsmart
by J.S. McDougall

Published by O'Reilly Media, Inc., 1005 Gravenstein Highway North, Sebastopol, CA 95472.

O'Reilly books may be purchased for educational, business, or sales promotional use. Online editions are also available for most titles (*http://my.safaribookson line.com*). For more information, contact our corporate/institutional sales department: (800) 998-9938 or *corporate@oreilly.com*.

Editor: Simon St. Laurent   **Cover Designer:** Susan Brown
Production Editor: Kristen Borg   **Interior Designer:** David Futato
Proofreader: O'Reilly Production Services **Illustrator:** Robert Romano

January 2012:   First Edition.

Revision History for the First Edition:
   2012-01-31   First release
See *http://oreilly.com/catalog/errata.csp?isbn=9781449309114* for release details.

ISBN: 978-1-449-30911-4

[LSI]

1328717386

For Dennis & Makenna.

Your love and support made this possible.

May you always walk with bears.

Table of Contents

Preface vii

1. The Radio Contest 1
    Advanced Strategies   3
        Landing a Big Fish   3
        Trivia Questions   4

2. The Tweet & Eat 5
    Advanced Strategies   7
        Secret Phrases   7
        Coupons   7

3. Hashtag Games 9
    Advanced Strategies   12
        Polling for a Winner   12

4. Twitter Market Research 13
    1. You Will Get an Answer   14
    2. Your Audience Will Invest Emotionally in You and Your
    Product   14

5. Twitter AdLibs 17
    Advanced Strategies   19

6. Twitter Haiku 21

7. Photo Caption Contest 25
    Advanced Strategies   26

8. **Treasure Hunt** **29**
Advanced Strategies   31
    Hot and Cold   31
    Prize Pirates   31

9. **Twitter BOGO—Buy One, Get One** **33**
Advanced Strategies   34
    Other Items   34
    Twitter Integration   34

10. **Discussion Groups** **37**

11. **Tweet Bombs** **39**
Advanced Strategies   40
    Tweet Bomb Prizes   40

12. **Web Scavenger Hunt** **41**

13. **Random Retweet** **45**
Advanced Strategies   46
    Nothing for Free   46
    Third Time's a Charm   46

14. **A Picture is Worth 7.14 Tweets** **47**

15. **The Star in the Crowd** **51**

16. **Digital Hide & Seek** **55**

17. **Smile. You're on Camera.** **57**

18. **Half-Off Hangman** **61**

19. **Topic Quotes** **65**

20. **Twitter Trivia** **67**

21. **Twitter Telephone** **69**

22. **Where In The World Is…?** **71**

23. I Feel So Close To You Right Now 75

24. I've Got The Golden Ticket! 79

25. Real-World Scavenger Hunt 83

Preface

Introduction

At nearly every conference I attend, I meet people who tell me, "I have no use for Twitter. You can't say anything in 140 characters. I'd rather have a *real* conversation." Obviously, as I'm the one writing this book, I feel differently. So, to all the doubters and skeptics, I offer the following story:

> My grandfather, "Mac" McDougall—like so many grandparents—moved to Florida when it came time for him to retire. His neighborhood was a flat rectangle, carved out of fields of orange groves, and tucked in beside a maze of golf courses. His street was a flat street in a grid of flat streets. His house was a single-level brown adobe home in a row of single-level brown adobe homes. At the end of his driveway was a green mailbox. At the end of every driveway was...a green mailbox.

> We would visit him nearly every winter. We'd often drive the long journey down I-95 from New Hampshire to Florida, and 24 hours after climbing into the van—as my dad drove the van through the flat streets—I would see my grandfather's house. Even as a small child, I had an easy time picking out his house from all the rest. His was the only one with a 50-foot radio tower standing in the backyard.

> My grandfather was a ham radio operator. He had received his operator's license in 1930 when he was just 15 years old. As a teenager, he taught himself how to build his own radios out of spare parts. He then served during WWII in a communications unit, and after the war he continued to communicate with other "hammers" all over the world. Upon retirement, he moved to this adobe home and set up his own radio room—complete with a radio tower outside his window.

> In the late evenings during our visits, he would excuse himself and shuffle to his radio room for his weekly appointments with his radio buddies. Sometimes I'd sit beside him—marveling at the knobs and lights all around the cluttered room—while he tapped out his messages in Morse code, laughed, and waited in anticipation for the beeps and boops that would reply.

> "Oh marvelous!" he'd say. "Janice had her baby!"

I—being six—didn't know Janice and didn't care much that she'd had her baby. But I could watch for hours as these sporadic beeps and boops somehow triggered outbursts of joy and happy tears from my grandfather.

I would learn many years later that my grandfather was speaking to a man in New Zealand named John. They met over the airwaves and quickly became friends—tapping back and forth to each other about their love of radios, golf, and the additions to their families.

Every week my grandfather would shuffle down the hall in the late evenings for his scheduled chat with John who—at that same time—was shuffling out of bed to start his day in New Zealand.

When my grandfather passed away in 2007, it had been over twenty years since I last sat with him in his radio room. At the time of his death he held the longest continuously-active ham radio operator license in the United States—77 years.

In a long procession on a sad day, we drove down the flat streets—past the orange groves and golf courses—to the funeral home. Family and friends filled the room, many of whom I hadn't seen in years and many of whom I'd never met. And, in introducing myself to some of the folks, I met a small white-haired man who stood alone at the back of the room. "Hello," he said in a funny accent. "I'm John."

Real relationships have been built on forms of communication offering far fewer than 140 characters. The human animal is capable of extracting real and meaningful information from countless forms of communication—whether it's Morse code, or a wink, a nervous foot, a billboard, or even a "tweet."

The content of your communication is important—not what carries it.

What This Book Is

This book is my answer to anyone who has ever asked the question, "OK. I've got my Twitter account...now what do I do?" In the following pages I have created 25 Twitter projects that will help you approach your Twitter community engagement efforts in a way that is strategic, fun, and measurable.

Too often people come up to me and say, "I set up my Twitter account. I was on there for a few weeks, and...it didn't really work." The rise of the planet's social media frenzy has spilled over into the business world. This frenzy has created a feeling in business owners and marketers that they need to be everywhere at once, all the time. This is crazy. People often create accounts on every new social media site that pops up, spend what precious little time they have in their day poking at it, and then leaving the account for dead when there are no immediate results. It's a common problem—and, being a small business owner myself, it's one with which I sympathize.

Consider this book your "Time out!"

The solution to this frenzied overexposure is not the automation of all 50 of your accounts. And the solution is not to work harder to try to keep up with all of them. To be effective at building an engaged community, businesses must slow down and work smarter.

Using focus, research, and a little strategy throughout your social media efforts, you will finally begin to see (and measure) some impressive results. The projects in this book will help you get started, but—in the end—I hope these are just training tools that will help you learn the elements of a successful campaign, and how to create campaigns all your own.

What This Book Is Not

This book is not a social media marketing manual. In fact, I shudder whenever I hear or use the phrase "social media marketing." *It just sounds slimy, doesn't it?* Twitter is not a marketing channel—and you should never view it as such.

These 25 projects are not "marketing projects." They are community-building projects. The goal of each of the following projects is to build an interested and engaged community for your business. The payoff that comes from having such a community around your business is increased sales, referrals, and opportunities for feedback and improvement. It is vital to understand the difference between your goal and your payoff.

Twitter is a community. Folks join Twitter to meet new friends and to discuss their interests with a wide variety of people—most of whom they will never meet in the real world. No one will ever tell you that they joined Twitter to make themselves more available to advertisers. Advertising on Twitter—sending out one-way, uninteresting, very short commercials for your stuff—will annoy people and you will be blocked, reported, and unfollowed. All of that is hard to wash off.

This book also won't walk you through the process of signing up for a Twitter account. There are many great books out there to help you do so. And, quite honestly, it isn't hard to figure out on your own.

But What If Twitter Goes Away?

As you know, the world of social media moves fast. The tools we use today will not be the tools we use tomorrow. MySpace was hot, and now it's gone. Friendster was popular, and now it's a memory. Twitter may well suffer the same fate. It could be replaced tomorrow by something new—and that's fine.

The tools we use may change—but the new mode of communication these tools have introduced is here to stay.

The lesson you take from this book should not be "how to use Twitter most effectively." The lesson is how to use these social tools to build, engage, and interact with your community. The ivory tower is gone in most industries. Social media makes CEOs accessible to the customers. This book should help you begin thinking about how best to create and capitalize on the opportunities presented by the leveling of the playing field.

How to Use This Book

The projects in this book have been written so that they are easy to follow and easy to replicate. I recommend you skim through each project until you find one that suits your comfort level and strikes you as both fun and possible given your audience and business. Then, just follow the steps I've laid out to get the wheels in motion.

The first few projects you attempt will likely fizzle out without any exciting explosion—and that's fine. It will take a while for you to work out the kinks and really begin to have a feel for how these strategies work. The first contest I ever ran was a miserable failure. In fact, the first few were. But, after a while, word caught on and people started showing up to play. Remember, this is not only new for you...the type of interaction will be new for your audience as well. Allow them time to catch on, get excited, and spread the word.

There are some easy projects in this book that require one person and a few minutes, and there are projects in here that will require considerably more time, people, and skill. Start with a few easy ones and then work your way up as you thirst for more of a challenge.

The QR Codes

Each project is accompanied by a QR code on the project's title page. Scan this QR code with your mobile device to recommend the project you're reading to your own followers. We're trying out a new print/Twitter integration in this book and we'd love it if you could give it a spin!

One final note: As I like to practice what I preach and I've long dreamed of making a "digital pop-up book," I've buried an easter egg somewhere within the book. Find it and let me know when you have. I can be reached on Twitter as @jsmcdougall. Happy hunting!

Conventions Used in This Book

The following typographical conventions are used in this book:

Italic
> Indicates new terms, URLs, email addresses, filenames, and file extensions.

`Constant width`
> Used for program listings, as well as within paragraphs to refer to program elements such as variable or function names, databases, data types, environment variables, statements, and keywords.

`Constant width bold`
> Shows commands or other text that should be typed literally by the user.

`Constant width italic`
> Shows text that should be replaced with user-supplied values or by values determined by context.

 This icon signifies a tip, suggestion, or general note.

 This icon indicates a warning or caution.

Using Code Examples

This book is here to help you get your job done. In general, you may use the code in this book in your programs and documentation. You do not need to contact us for permission unless you're reproducing a significant portion of the code. For example, writing a program that uses several chunks of code from this book does not require permission. Selling or distributing a CD-ROM of examples from O'Reilly books does require permission. Answering a question by citing this book and quoting example code does not require permission. Incorporating a significant amount of example code from this book into your product's documentation does require permission.

We appreciate, but do not require, attribution. An attribution usually includes the title, author, publisher, and ISBN. For example: "*#tweetsmart* by J.S. McDougall (O'Reilly). Copyright 2012 J.S. McDougall, 978-1-449-30911-4."

If you feel your use of code examples falls outside fair use or the permission given above, feel free to contact us at *permissions@oreilly.com*.

Safari® Books Online

 Safari Books Online is an on-demand digital library that lets you easily search over 7,500 technology and creative reference books and videos to find the answers you need quickly.

With a subscription, you can read any page and watch any video from our library online. Read books on your cell phone and mobile devices. Access new titles before they are available for print, and get exclusive access to manuscripts in development and post feedback for the authors. Copy and paste code samples, organize your favorites, download chapters, bookmark key sections, create notes, print out pages, and benefit from tons of other time-saving features.

O'Reilly Media has uploaded this book to the Safari Books Online service. To have full digital access to this book and others on similar topics from O'Reilly and other publishers, sign up for free at *http://my.safaribooksonline.com*.

How to Contact Us

Please address comments and questions concerning this book to the publisher:

O'Reilly Media, Inc.
1005 Gravenstein Highway North
Sebastopol, CA 95472
800-998-9938 (in the United States or Canada)
707-829-0515 (international or local)
707-829-0104 (fax)

We have a web page for this book, where we list errata, examples, and any additional information. You can access this page at:

http://shop.oreilly.com/product/0636920021315.do

To comment or ask technical questions about this book, send email to:

bookquestions@oreilly.com

For more information about our books, courses, conferences, and news, see our website at *http://www.oreilly.com*.

Find us on Facebook: *http://facebook.com/oreilly*

Follow us on Twitter: *http://twitter.com/oreillymedia*

Watch us on YouTube: *http://www.youtube.com/oreillymedia*

CHAPTER 1

The Radio Contest

This is the first project in the book for two reasons: it is simple for beginners; and it is special to me. This project explains how to run the same contest on Twitter that provided me with my "A-HA!" moment. Like many people, I was originally skeptical that business and social media could mix. Like I said in the Introduction, I still shudder when I hear or use the phrase "social media marketing." This contest proved to me that the two worlds could collide—and that the result can be spectacular.

Tweet This...

This contest is a adaptation of the old "Be the 10th caller"-style contest radio stations have been running for decades. However, instead of asking people to call in, we're asking people to send tweets. So, in effect, this is a "Be the 10th tweeter"-style contest.

For the price of some sort of prize—a coupon, a product, a free hour of service, etc.—you can use this contest to directly engage your audience with your products and services—and in doing so, recommend you to their followers.

The idea is simple: at the same time every week, invite your followers into your online store or website and ask them to tweet out a link to the product of yours they'd like to win. The 10th (or 12th or 50th, etc.) person to send such a tweet after the defined time, wins the product he or she has chosen.

Before you can run the actual contest, you will need to do some preparation work in order for it to be most effective.

Choose a time you will run the contest every week. Plan to do it during the work day, as that's when most people are at their computers and looking for something to do (or trying to avoid something they don't want to do). Be sure to run the contest at the same time every week so that your followers can plan to show up and play regularly.

The first step is to place a "Tweet This" button on all the product and/or service pages on your website that you'd like to make available for the contest. If you're using a modern content management system (CMS) like WordPress or Drupal to manage your site, you will likely only need to update one product page template file.

Using the HTML code Twitter provides through their Tweet button creation tool (*http://twitter.com/goodies*), create the JavaScript code you will need to copy and paste into your website's HTML. Fill in the field that designates that the button should include your username in each tweet sent. This will allow you to track the tweets your followers send from your site.

This button will give your visitors the ability to recommend your individual products or service out to their followers with a simple click of the new button on any product's page.

Once the button is installed and functioning, write a blog post that explains the rules and the workings of the contest. When it comes time to promote the contest, you can point people to the blog post where everything is laid out and made clear.

In the hours before the designated time you've chosen to run the contest, promote the contest every so often by tweeting out a link to the blog post you've written. Do not overdo it. It's easy to get excited and overpromote the contest, but annoying your followers with constant promotion will only turn them off. Use a light touch.

Also, when promoting the contest, don't just stick to Twitter. Try to enlist the help of bloggers, Facebook users, and newsletter owners you know who might be interested in helping you promote the contest. A well-placed and well-timed article about your contest can bring in a good number of new people.

The blog post you've written explaining the contest should invite people to browse through your online store in the minutes before the contest is scheduled to start—let's say, for the sake of example, the contest is run every Tuesday at 2 o'clock. In the minutes before the contest is to start, visitors will enter your store and begin looking for a product they would like to win that week. When 2 o'clock rolls around, send out a tweet announcing that the contest has started and that anyone browsing the store should begin clicking the "Tweet This" button on the page of the product they hope to win.

You, as the contest manager, can track these tweets by running a search for your username at *http://search.twitter.com* or through Twitter management software like TweetDeck (*http://www.tweetdeck.com*) or HootSuite (*http://www.hootsuite.com*). As the tweets start flying, you begin counting. When you have counted up to the 10th tweeter, you have your winner and the contest for the week is over. Announce the winner and the prize, and thank everybody for playing.

Contact the winner directly—usually via a direct message—to send your congratulations and request his mailing address and other required information. Plop the prize in the mail and you're done!

In the early weeks of running this contest, you can expect low numbers and slow response rates. You might have four or five people play in the first week, and therefore you should set your "Be the 'Nth' tweeter" number low. Every week however, because the participants are recommending you out to their followers in their contest tweets, your contest numbers will grow. In a few weeks' time, you can expect 30 to 40 people participating in your contest every week.

I realize that 30 to 40 people does not sound like many participants. But, keep in mind that during the course of the 10-minute contest, each of those 30 to 40 people is sending out a tweet with a link back to your site to all of their followers to read. When gauging the effectiveness of your contest, add up not only the number of folks who played, but also the number of folks who received the tweeted link recommendations. You will be astonished how quickly you can reach 20,000 (or more) people with only a few dozen people participating in your contest.

Advanced Strategies

Once you've been doing this contest for a few months and you feel as though you've got a handle on how it works, there are a few things you can do to improve its effectiveness.

Landing a Big Fish

It is great to get a bunch of individuals and loyal customers to participate in your contest, but it is even better to get some powerhouse Twitter users who operate in your niche to play along as well.

For example, if you own a shoe store and use the contest to give away a free pair of shoes every week, you should try to get the Twitter marketers at companies like Runner's World magazine, Dr. Scholl's, or even Nike to play along as well. These companies often have large numbers of followers and are often more than willing to participate in a fun contest that suits their audience. This is a quick way to double or triple the number of people playing in the contest —and the more people who play, the more promotion your contest gets, and the more people who play...and so on.

Trivia Questions

If you run this contest the same way every week, it won't take long for it to become stale and less interesting for your audiences. Therefore, you should spice it up every so often by throwing in a fun bonus question. In this iteration of the contest, you would give away two prizes—one to the normal contest winner, but also one to the first person to answer the bonus question correctly.

Along with every bonus question, you might want to provide a link to a page on your website—or another appropriate (or fun) website, where the participants can find the answer.

For example, during your shoe store's contest one week, you could provide a link to your own site's About Us page—which contains a long description of each of your office dogs—along with the question, "Of the four dogs in our office, which little ball of sunshine ate my $300 Nikes?!"

This type of question draws people to your site's About Us page, where they learn that your company is run by humans with a sense of humor—which is always a good thing for your customers to learn.

CHAPTER 2

The Tweet & Eat

I've had the idea for this project bouncing around in the back of my head for a few years. It first came to me when I was probably hungry, and watching the "Inspired Burrito" restaurant chain Boloco (@boloco) interact with their audience on Twitter. Boloco is a relatively new burrito restaurant chain that started in Boston, Massachusetts, and they do a great job of customer care on Twitter.

I went to school in Boston for a few years and even though Twitter didn't exist when I was in school, I thought it would have been cool if such a restaurant used social media to get Boston's huge and hungry student population out of their dorms and engaging with their food out in the world. Hence, this idea for the Tweet & Eat was born.

This project can work with any number of different types of businesses, but I always see it working most effectively with hungry college students, and therefore I will use a fictional burrito place as an example—NOT Boloco, of course, as I don't want to play favorites. (Hi @Boloco!)

Try it out for yourself and riff as needed.

This project makes use of what I think to be the most powerful and most interesting potential of social media—audience engagement and interaction in the real world. In this project you will pack your goodies—whether burritos, or hats, or books—into a vehicle and drive them into the nearest city or town with your desired audience. Tweet clues to your location and the first X number of people to sleuth you out will win those free goodies, and meet some very nice business owners.

So let's say you're the owner of The Wicked Awesome Burrito House and you're having trouble drawing in orders from the hungry local student population—which is your target demographic. Running this sort of real-world Tweet & Eat game on Twitter may help attract attention from the young audience, raise awareness of your burritos within that audience, and engage the students in a way that is fun and free (for them).

The first thing to do is to write up a blog post on your website explaining the rules, the Tweet & Eat's hashtag, the schedule, and the prizes for finding you. Plan for a day when a lot of college kids (and other people) would be out and about—maybe a Saturday in the summer or homecoming weekend.

In the week before the Tweet & Eat is to take place, promote the event by sending tweets, posting the link to the blog post on Facebook, and sending out e-newsletters. You should also spend some time promoting the Tweet & Eat in the real world as well by printing flyers for all of your restaurant locations, local colleges' bulletin boards, telephone poles, dorms, and anywhere else you can slam a staple without getting arrested.

On the day of the Tweet & Eat, pack up a bunch of your most popular burritos (or what have you) into the van's warming tray, and head out into your local town or city. Park the van on a busy street and hide out while you tweet your clues from your mobile device.

The clues you tweet should be fun and possible to figure out. Take and tweet photos of interesting architecture near where you've parked; send out riddle-like questions about the name of the street you're on; if you're feeling bookish, send out historical facts about the part of the city you're in. Be sure to use the unifying hashtag in all of your tweets so that you can see and respond to all of the people participating.

Once people have found you, break out the burritos and begin the swingin' sidewalk burrito party. Word of your hot freebies and fun Tweet & Eat adventure will spread quickly throughout the hungry burrito-loving population. And soon your van's burrito warmer will have been cleaned out, you will have introduced your burritos to new customers, and you will have created a fun afternoon that people will be telling their friends about.

This type of real-world interaction breaks a few barriers that often stand in the way of people trying something new. First of all, you've approached your audience in way that is safe and familiar to them—via Twitter. Second, you've offered up a fun and engaging way to try your products, food, and services. And finally, you have offered a risk-free method for trying new things. As you know, consumers often stick to what they know will be reliable. People fall into ruts because walking into a new place often doesn't seem worth the risk.

This type of interaction will pull the local eating, consuming, and buying population out of their ruts and into your restaurant or location.

Advanced Strategies

Secret Phrases

On the radio, you'll often hear DJs asking their listeners to call up with the "Phrase that Pays!" This is a way to differentiate callers who have been listening to the promotions from the people who are just calling up anyway. In this project, to make things more exciting, you could incorporate a secret phase, a secret knock, or even a secret dance that the seekers would need to reveal once they find your hiding place. In the example above, this would help you differentiate the folks who followed the Twitter Tweet & Eat from the folks who just stumbled upon some strange people in a van giving out free burritos.

Coupons

It would not be any fun for your followers to chase Twitter clues for a few hours in an afternoon only to succeed and walk away with a few crummy coupons. (There's an epidemic of coupon tweets taking over Twitter. But more on that later.) Coupons are great tools for giving folks an incentive to visit your store, office, restaurant, or location, but—in this case—it cannot be the only prize. Use coupons as an incentive to get the people to come visit you later at your store only *after* they've gobbled up your main prize.

Hashtag Games

Twitter uses a system of hashtags to organize the millions of conversations that are all happening simultaneously. A hashtag is a keyword or phrase preceded by the pound sign: #.

Twitter's system of hashtags is an organic creation —invented not by Twitter, but by Twitter-user Chris Messina in August of 2007—to help users organize their conversations around topic areas. There is no hashtag registration process. There is no monitoring service. People create and insert hashtags into their messages as they please for a number of different reasons.

If you've spent any time on Twitter, you've no doubt seen them in the wild already. People sometimes append them to their messages to indicate the type of message.

"President signs historic bill into law. #breaking #news"

Or, sometimes people work the hashtag into the text of their message:

"OMG I think an #earthquake just rumbled through town."

Either way, the authors of these messages are using hashtags to ensure that their messages show up in a larger stream of messages devoted to the topic represented by each included hashtag.

When readers of Twitter messages care to peek in on what people are currently saying on any given topic, they can simply run a search for a particular hashtag. Searching for #earthquake, for example, will alert the reader instantly to reactions from people about any seismic activity around the globe. A search for #breaking will produce a stream of messages from people discussing the latest breaking news. And so on.

Often, people use hashtags as commentary. This is a lighthearted way to insert some sideways jabs of ancillary thoughts into Twitter messages. For example:

> "Just watched 'Dude Where's My Car?' Ashton Kutcher for the Oscar! #whenpigsfly"
> "Left my camera on the roof of my car and drove away. #bonehead"

And finally, people use hashtags to organize fun word challenges—which is what we'll be discussing in this project.

Twitter word games are fun and customizable projects to do with your followers. They can be particularly effective when mixed with some bawdy or self-deprecating humor.

For example, one of the most popular hashtag games out there is "Movie Titles that Sound Dirty, But Aren't" or #movietitlesthatsounddirtybutarent. In this game, folks comb through their mental movie libraries, their DVD collections, IMDb, their Netflix queue, or wherever they want in order to come up with movie titles that are funny when viewed through a not-so-classy lens.

 There are no capitalization rules when it comes to hashtags. The only limitation in creating a hashtag is that the hashtag cannot contain spaces or punctuation. So, if you think the capitalized version (#MovieTitlesThatSoundDirtyButArent) is easier to read, go for it. Just be aware that some people will use the all-lowercase version, and that's OK.

Here are some classic participant offerings:

> "Full Frontal #movietitlesthatsounddirtybutarent"
> "A Few Good Men #movietitlesthatsounddirtybutarent"
> "Driving Miss Daisy #movietitlesthatsounddirtybutarent"

Yes, they're gross. But also hilarious.

Another popular variation of this hashtag game is to ask folks to offer up classic book titles with one word of the title changed to a predetermined word—and therefore changing the connotation of the title entirely.

For example, a possible hashtag game might be "Book Titles with One Word Changed to Odor" or #booktitleswithonewordchangedtoodor.

> "Zen and the Odor of Motorcycle Maintenance #booktitleswithoneword-changedtoodor"
> "Odors with Morrie #booktitleswithonewordchangedtoodor"
> "Pride and Odor #booktitleswithonewordchangedtoodor"
> "The Da Vinci Odor #booktitleswithonewordchangedtoodor"

Your version of the game can be less...bawdy than my examples—but be sure not to get so serious that it's not funny! People will only play along if it's fun to do so.

So, how do you make these Twitter hashtag word games work for you? Simple. You just need to invent your own word game based on your company, products, or topic area. You know your audience best, so invent a word game that will pique their interest as well as reinforce your position as a leader in your niche.

Say, for example, that you work for Harvard Common Press—a publisher of wonderful cookbooks. You could start a game called "Harvard Common Book Titles in Bed" or #harvardcommonbooktitlesinbed. The purpose of this game is to ask your audience to find the funniest combinations of one of your book titles and the words "in bed."

Here are some possible entries (for fictional book titles):

"From Frozen to Full in Under 5 Minutes in bed #harvardcommonbooktitlesinbed"
"The Grill Master's Guide to Meat in bed #harvardcommonbooktitlesinbed"
"The Wine Lover in You in bed #harvardcommonbooktitlesinbed"

This game accomplishes a few things. First, it's hilarious and your audience will appreciate that you are a human with a sense of humor. Second, the game spreads your name and your book titles out to the millions of the people on Twitter. Each time someone submits an entry, your company name and one of your book titles are sent to people who have never heard of you before. Third, and most importantly, the game encourages participants to browse through your bookstore looking for potentially funny book titles, and therefore your audience will become more familiar with your products.

If you're not a publisher and don't have a library of book or movie titles to work with, here are a few other ideas to kick-start your brainstorming process. Remember, you're not limited to toying with your own products. Investigate other aspects of your company or your topic area as well for interesting games to play.

- Restaurants and bars could offer up the names of their cocktails, dishes, or desserts.
- A local ski shop could play a game riffing on the names of the world's most famous skiers, ski movies, or ski resorts.
- A knitting magazine could play games with the names of various stitches used in the craft.

With a little thought and exploration, you'll be able to come up with a good number of fun games to play that your specific audience will enjoy.

Advanced Strategies

Polling for a Winner

To make the game more interesting, you can add some competition into the mix by asking your audience not only to contribute entries, but to vote on a winner. There are a couple ways to do this.

The first and simplest way to collect votes is to use a Twitter polling service, such as TwtPoll. You will need to create the poll and load in the contest entries. Once created, the polling service will provide you with a shortened URL that you can send out to all your followers. Ask them to submit their vote for the best of the bunch.

The second, and most public, way to collect votes is to ask your audience to simply retweet their favorite entry. You will need to count up all the retweets of all the individual entries, but all the extra publicity created by all the extra retweeting should make up for the extra work.

It's up to you whether or not you'd like to offer up a prize for the winning entry. My advice is to gauge your audience and—if you do choose to give something away—make the prize small. The goal of this game is not to start a voting war among your audience members. The goal is to engage the entire audience in a fun and genuine way.

CHAPTER 4

Twitter Market Research

Your Twitter audience can offer you far more than just sales and community. If you put aside your sales goals and profit and loss statements for a moment, you should begin to see the not-so-obvious benefits that come from having a collection of thousands, or tens of thousands, of instantly contactable people at your disposal—each of whom is familiar with your company.

You work every day to make great products or provide great services. It's a struggle—I know!—and you have to make decisions every day that will impact your customers. Often, the right answer is not obvious—would folks prefer a red option or a green? Chocolate or strawberry? This title or that title?

Many companies spend millions of dollars polling, polling, polling the general public hoping to find an answer that will recoup the millions of dollars they've spent in asking the questions. It's a risky proposition. However, while large companies will always find reasons to spend millions of dollars on market research, you don't have to. You have a targeted and engaged Twitter audience packed with your ideal customers. Therefore, when you're faced with making a tough decision that will affect your customers (and your sales), you have the luxury of being able to plain-ol' ask them for their preference.

This is the purest form of customer engagement. Invite your followers into your decision-making process. This strategy will accomplish several things.

1. You Will Get an Answer

No matter your question—whether it's "What should we title this book?" or "What color do you want for a vacuum cleaner?" or "Which logo do you like better?"—you will get plenty of feedback. You may choose to use the feedback you receive—or you may choose to junk it—but you will be able to base your decisions on the opinions of the people who are most likely to buy (and recommend) your product.

If the question is simple, it should be simple for people to answer you. You don't have to (and shouldn't) go to lengthy extremes to set up a response collection mechanism. If you've got a simple question, think of this approach as sticking your finger in the wind. You don't want to ask people to go through a lengthy survey process when all they need to do is give you a one-word reply: "Green."

If you've got multiple questions—or you really want to dig into market research—you can absolutely set up a sophisticated (and simple to use) response collection mechanism. There are plenty of wonderful services out there that will help you do this—SurveyMonkey, Wufoo, TwtSurvey, etc. Find a service that will let you organize and present the questions in a way that will appeal, and make sense to, your audience. Once you've created the survey, send a message to your followers with the question (or a teaser question) and a link to where they can submit their reply. Your response rates will be lower with this method than with quick questions asked and answered via Twitter, but you should still be able to collect enough data to make it worthwhile.

2. Your Audience Will Invest Emotionally in You and Your Product

When you invite people into your decision-making process, you're giving them a peek behind the curtain—and therefore you've provided your Twitter followers with special access that the general public may not receive. This peek is valuable—and therefore your followers are less likely to unfollow you out of boredom or disinterest, and are more likely to recommend you to their like-minded friends.

By inviting people into your decision-making process, you're allowing your audience to become emotionally invested in the product or project on which you're working. They will, therefore, be more interested in reading about the product's release or the project's launch—saying, "I chose that green!" or "They picked the right logo!" or, more likely, "My title was way better!"

Remember, soliciting feedback doesn't lock you into using it. Design by committee does not produce genius. But, any way you slice it, involving your Twitter followers in your process will build more of a relationship with your most-likely customers than ever could have been built with a press release or commercial.

CHAPTER 5

Twitter AdLibs

MadLibs! You know 'em. You love 'em. Those outrageous and compelling fill-in-the-blank games always lead to the funniest (and usually grossest) places. Lucky for us, the game's short format translates well to Twitter and can be a _____ load of fun!

Tweet This...

To prepare for this game, create a list of quotes or sentences or one-liners that relate to your products, services, company, or topic area. You could also grab a full paragraph of text from your website, your mission statement, your company bio, your product descriptions, etc. Strategically remove a few key words from every sentence where you think substitute words could have the funniest effect.

For example, here's an excerpt from my bio on the website for Catalyst Webworks. (I'll use my own so as not to risk offending anyone else.)

> Jesse has over 12 years of experience as a web designer, programmer, and web strategist. He speaks about web marketing at conferences across the country. Jesse is the author of eight books about conducting business on the web.

The tweets you send out should look something like this—use the underscore to signify the blank spaces, and number your messages if the sentences you're sending combine into one full paragraph.

> "Jesse has over 12 _____ of _____ as a web designer, programmer, and _____. #adlibs 1/3"
> "He _____ about web marketing at _____ across the country. #adlibs 2/3"
> "Jesse is the _____ of _____ books about _____ _____ on the web. #adlibs 3/3"

Due to the length of each sentence in the paragraph, you will need to send out each as its own tweet. Challenge your audience to fill in the blanks in the funniest way possible.

Obviously, the replies you receive will range from "actually smart and witty" to "...dude, you should be in some sort of facility." So be prepared for some un-funny and off-color humor to emerge from the depths of Twitter. And, as this is the case, be sure to use only company bios or information that you (and the rest of the company) feels good about having some fun with.

The format of the replies coming back to you will vary. Some people will retype the entire sentence, having filled in the blanks:

> "Jesse has over 12 minutes of fumbling as a web designer, programmer, and shotputter. #adlibs 1/3"

While others—due to space constraints—will have just sent you the substituted words:

> "renowned collector / 10,000 / dancing / bananas #adlibs 3/3"

One of Twitter's greatest features is also one of its greatest failings: the messages posted tend not to remain visible for very long. Therefore, if you receive great responses to your #adlibs, you might want to pull them off Twitter and post them to someplace more substantial—like your company blog, your Facebook wall, or Tumblr, for example. This way, the fruits of your labor and the wit of your audience can be better enjoyed and shared. This is where numbering your messages (1/4, 2/4, 3/4, etc.) comes in handy. When you repost to your blog, you will need the numbers to complete the full sentence:

> "Jesse is the renowned collector of 10,000 books about dancing bananas on the web. #adlibs 3/3"

If you would rather not get into the bother of piecing back together full paragraphs, it's possible to have a great time with this project even if you choose to tweet out only single sentences. It's fun to use phrases that will be familiar to your audience—such as your motto, mission statement, book titles, menu items, product names, etc.

> "Gee, your _____ smells _____! #adlibs"
> "I can't _____ it's not _____! #adlibs"
> "We craft _____ and _____. And we have a _____ _____ doing it. #adlibs"
> "The _____-Hour _____ Week #adlibs"

If you do choose to repost responses to your blog, write out the ones that have been truncated due to space constraints, and be sure to credit the authors properly. This will help you with promotion when your followers want to send all their friends a link to where you've posted that funny thing they said.

Advanced Strategies

If you wish to stay even more true to the original game, you could suggest which of the eight parts of speech you'd like for people to provide for the blanks. This will change the format of your tweets a bit. Instead of using only solid underscores—which take up a good amount of space—you'll need to downsize and be more specific:

> "He [verb] about web marketing at [noun] across the country. #adlibs 2/3"

The advantage of this method is that you are more closely able to control they type of responses you'll receive, and you will get to have the pleasure of revisiting your old grammar lessons. Here's a hint:

- Noun: any abstract or concrete entity
- Pronoun: any substitute for a noun or noun phrase
- Adjective: any qualifier of a noun
- Verb: any action or state of being
- Adverb: any qualifier of an adjective, verb, or other adverb
- Preposition: any establisher of relation and syntactic context
- Conjunction: any syntactic connector
- Interjection: any emotional greeting (or "exclamation")

So, for example:

> "[interjection]! Jesse [verb] at making [adjective] [noun]! #adlib"

The replies, of course, would look something like this:

> "Wow! Jesse excels at making Twitter fun! #adlib"
> "Crap! Jesse sucks at making tasty banana bread. #adlib"
> "Geez! Jesse rocks at making grammar lessons. #adlib"

Grammar modifies lessons, Twitter modifies fun, and bananas make everything better. #pow

CHAPTER 6

Twitter Haiku

Haiku! The ancient form of poetry that has thrilled 8- and 80-year-olds for centuries has found a new fan base on one of the world's newest communication platforms. Haiku's short format has made haiku the poetry of choice for folks limited to only 140 characters.

Haiku, as you may know, is a form of poem consisting of three lines with 17 total syllables, in a 5/7/5 syllable configuration. These strict rules make writing good haiku wickedly hard. But, it also makes writing bad haiku wonderfully fun. Tossing around topic-based haikus is the perfect Twitter pastime, and it's a great intellectual exercise with which to challenge your brilliant Twitter community.

To get started with this project, first define your hashtag. It should be a word or short phrase that is easily recognizable to your audience, followed by the word 'haiku.'

For example, if your business is selling ugly Christmas sweaters to the seasonally jovial, you could use the hashtag: #uglyxmassweaterhaiku. Or, if you run a pet store, you could appeal to the common experiences of pet owners: #whenmydogwasapuppyhaiku. Or, maybe you run an airline: #thingsnottodowhileflyinghaiku. Try to find a fun theme for your haiku project that will encourage your followers to play along.

Once you've chosen your theme, write up a quick blog post explaining the concept to your audience—as this type of Twitter interaction may be new to them—and offer up a sample haiku.

Let say, for the sake of example, that you own a pet store. Your first haikus could be:

"Pee on the sofa / Torn slippers in the hallway / Totally worth it #whenmydogwasapuppyhaiku"

"Hey, what's over here? / Hey, what's that over this way? / Now back over here? #goldfishinabowlhaiku"

"Hello. Hello. Squawk! / Does Polly want a cracker?! / Goodbye. Squawk! Goodbye! #every2minutesinapetstorehaiku"

Or, if you sell ugly Christmas sweaters.

"Blinking Santa Claus / battery-powered music / my Christmas sweater #uglyxmassweaterhaiku"

"Went to a party / spilled egg nog on my sweater / nobody noticed #uglyxmassweaterhaiku"

"Make sweaters all year / fringe, tassles, ornaments, glue / sell out in three days #uglyxmassweaterhaiku"

Or, if you run an airline:

"30,000 feet / 200 people in back / whisky calms the nerves #thingsnottodowhileflyinghaiku"

"Bags to Miami / Bags to Denver and Spokane / Plane to Chicago #hownottorunanairlinehaiku"

"Plane now arriving / at gate 10...11...12 / Who oiled the runway? #airlinehijinxhaiku"

Twitter Haiku tends to be one of the longest-running games that people play. Therefore, it is very well-suited to longer-running promotional campaigns like event promotion:

"The creative world / freed from the cubicle farm / can't wait for #moocon! #mooconhaiku"

"Seminars and cheese / massages, food, no wifi / #moocon 2012! #mooconhaiku"

"Alone in a field / with all my creative friends / making what we love #mooconhaiku"

Or, for product launches:

"drag-and-drop uploads / fly-out menus, bug fixes / WordPress 3.3 #wp33haiku"

"hot and spicy food / the best barbecue ever / hot and spicy chef #thenewbbqbookhaiku"

"it runs on solar / it recaptures momentum / and the brakes will work #thenewpriushaiku"

But Twitter Haiku is at its best when the entire community begins to participate. So, when designing your haiku project, try to choose a theme that will encourage others to play along.

For example, you could solicit feedback from your audience in the form of haiku:

- Product reviews:

  "Love my Toyota / 500 miles from each tank / wish it came in green #toyotareviewhaiku"

- Or photo captions—after tweeting a photo of one of your products—maybe a pair of your hiking boots on a cat:

  "Clomp. Clomp. Clomp. Meow. / I always thought Puss in Boots / wasn't a real cat. #timberlandcaptionhaiku"

- Or feature requests:

  "Your software is great / but I need a button for / applied logistics #appliedlogisticsfeaturehaiku"

As you can see, there are a lot of great ways to incorporate haiku into your Twitter time. Once you get the ball rolling, and your audience is well-versed in the ways of the game, new haiku games will arise from your audience organically—and you'll have a great time.

CHAPTER 7

Photo Caption Contest

People love eye candy, brain teasers, lighthearted competition, and belly laughs. This next project combines all those elements into one engaging Twitter project: a photo caption contest. This is a great project because it provides you with plenty of opportunities for both driving web traffic and targeted product promotion—all while having a great time with your followers.

To start this project you'll need a photo. The photo you choose will determine the goals of your project.

If you're pressed for time and would just like to run a quick and lighthearted caption contest, you can grab any old image off the web that appeals to your audience—a chef making a funny face, an upside-down puppy, a sneaker in a mud puddle. If you spend some time combing Google Images or Flickr or iStockphoto, you'll be able to find a curious or funny image to use.

If you've got some time to play with—and a camera at your disposal—I recommend taking some time to create your own photo. This photo could be a shot of one of your products in a curious setting, or your CEO making a funny face, or a manipulated image of King Kong sitting on top of your office building. This image should, in a fun way, incorporate your topic, products, company, location, or brand. Take the extra time to make it stand out—it will only help you with referrals.

Once you've found your photo, post it to your blog with a write-up of the contest rules. The rules are up to you, but I do recommend that you define a hashtag for the contest so that you can track entries.

If you wish, you can raise the stakes by giving away a prize to the author of the funniest submission. Or, you can just run the contest for the fun of it. If you choose to select a winner, you can do so either by executive order (you just pick your favorite), or you can use a more democratic approach by asking your followers to retweet their favorites.

Once the photo and contest rules are complete and public, it is time to begin the contest! Send out a tweet announcing the contest and linking to your blog post. Be sure to include the hashtag.

> "Our photo caption contest! Just what is CEOTim thinking while on that unicycle?! *http://jmcd.me/zZJ1IO* #oreillycaptioncontest"

Collect and post a gallery of the responses to your blog, Tumblr, Flickr, etc. This public display of entries will encourage new followers to join in the fun, and—because everyone on Twitter wants more followers—posting the usernames of your participants will give them much-desired exposure to new people.

In addition to posting entries to your blog, be sure to retweet some of them as well—including a link back to the gallery.

Once the contest has run its course, or has reached the deadline you set, declare a winner—if you've chosen to do so—and thank everyone for their submissions!

Advanced Strategies

The photo you use in your contest provides a great opportunity to highlight a particular product or person. It is also a good place to show some love back to your followers. One great variation on this contest is to solicit photos from your followers in preparation for the contest. You could have a pre-contest contest to determine which photo you're going to use.

To make sure you get photos you can actually use, it's best to have some pretty strict parameters for eligible photos. You don't want every one of your Twitter followers sending you photos of their cat sneezing. You want photos that re-inforce your brand, your community, or your place as an expert in your niche.

Here are some types of photos you could request from your followers:

- Photos of your products in your followers' homes
- Photos of your website on laptops or mobile devices in exotic locations
- Photos of your company sticker in odd places
- Photos of your followers wearing your company apparel
- Photos of your followers wearing a fake tattoo of your logo
- Photos of your followers interacting in some way with your products

This approach is a wonderful way to get people interacting with your stuff out in the real world. And, obviously, this strategy is easier if you've been giving out hats, t-shirts, fake tattoos, and stickers for the last decade.

CHAPTER 8

Treasure Hunt

Want to know what's more fun than a treasure hunt? Well, I'll tell you. *Nothing.*

This project is a favorite of mine. It—like all my favorites—combines the power of Twitter with action in the real world. There's something so satisfying about turning tweets into motion. Whenever I watch a Twitter treasure hunt or some similar project that's got people running all around, I'm always reminded of being eleven years old and talking to my brothers and friends over our cheap

Tweet This...

walkie-talkies. Even though we were just playing in the woods behind our suburban house, with these "global" communication devices, we could inspire, organize, and mobilize great imaginary campaigns. We would hunt for treasure, storm distant battlefields, and perform clandestine reconnaissance missions to save our little sister from the sandbox—all before it was time for our olive-loaf sandwiches. #omnomnom

This project captures that spirit of youth and combines it with cut-throat consumerist bargain-hunting. What could be better?!

In this project you're playing the role of a bumbling pirate who has buried (and lost) some treasure in the world. And, since we're dealing with hiding some actual physical goods in this case, this project is best performed in a well-defined physical location—such as at a mall, shopping plaza, city center, school, trade show, or conference.

The concept is simple. You, as the organizer, hide something of value somewhere within the event or venue. Then, when everybody has collected for the conference or event—or you have enough of a crowd at the mall or store—begin tweeting out your clever clues to the item's location using an appropriate hashtag.

If you're running this project at a conference, use the conference's hashtag in addition to a hashtag devoted to the treasure hunt. For example, if you were to run such a treasure hunt at the annual SXSW conference, you would say something like:

> "I'm hiding where everyone is looking, but where no one will see. #sxswtreasurehunt #sxsw"

Using the two separate hashtags in this case ensures that your tweets are seen by everybody following the conference's general Twitter stream, as well as everybody who wants to follow the treasure hunt exclusively. If you only used #sxswtreasurehunt, no one except your followers and those "in-the-know" would know to follow it—most people at the conference would miss out.

Stand in a central location, if possible, so you get to watch all the fun of people scurrying about looking under potted plants, behind mannequins, in the fountains, and under the elderly. Encourage folks to send you questions as they are running about. These questions, which you can choose either to answer or ignore, will provide you with opportunities to steer the mob. If the venue is giant, people are way off course, or you have a lunch date with a model, you could hurry things along by replying to the calls for help with additional riddles.

> "From where I peek, I see 1000 faces, and you only see one. #sxsw treasurehunt #sxsw"

When a person stumbles upon your hiding spot, the prize should have a tag on it that contains the "Winning phrase!" In order to claim the prize, the person who discovered the prize will need to tweet the message. This phrase should be unique to each treasure hunt and will confirm for you, while you're at lunch with that model, that someone has finally discovered the prize. The phrase should be something fun and promotional.

> "I won! Some say bears go 'round smelling bad, but I found the teddy bear behind the screen! #sxsw #sxswtreasurehunt http://jmcd.me/zvf0zW"

Once someone has found the prize, be sure to send thanks, congratulations, and details about the next treasure hunt. This project, like the "Be the 10th Caller" project, is most effective when you play at a regularly scheduled time and place.

Advanced Strategies

Hot and Cold

If you're feeling frisky, or want to liven things up a bit, you could play the "Hot & Cold" game while watching people run around the venue. If someone is getting close to your hiding spot and you know who it is, you could call out on Twitter that they're getting warmer.... If you don't know the usernames of the folks playing along, you could use a description of the person or their clothing, instead of a username.

"Someone in seafoam pants and a hot pink flamingo shirt is getting awfully warm right now....! #sxsw #sxswtreasurehunt"

This is a quick way to enliven the atmosphere as people run about.

Prize Pirates

If you would like to enlist your friends or staff to help you run the game, you could designate some helper pirates to stand at strategic points around the venue with a set of additional pre-written riddles and a bucket full of trinket prizes or gift certificates. In addition to hunting for the grand prize, folks playing along could happen across one of these guest Prize Pirates—possibly dressed in tri-corner hats—and request the riddle. If the riddle is answered correctly, that pirate's small prize is awarded. Obviously, this strategy would work best in a large venue where you could space out your Prize Pirates a bit.

CHAPTER 9

Twitter BOGO—Buy One, Get One

Here's a simple project you can do with your audience that will directly spur sales AND free promotion of your products. This project leans a bit toward the conventional marketing side of the social media marketing spectrum, which makes it somewhat riskier for you than the projects focused exclusively on community-building. But, if you make this one funny or fun, I don't think you'll run into any pushback from your audience. Plus—remember the golden rule—people *love* freebies.

Discounting is a great way to grab attention and move product. "Buy one, get one free" sales (or BOGO) are pretty easy in a retail store: the customer buys a pair of shoes, and you hand the customer another pair. On the web, however, it can be difficult to pull off. E-commerce platforms and shopping cart software are expensive to customize, and rarely have advanced selling techniques built-in. Your options for running a sale are usually limited to defining a category, a time period, and a discounted percentage.

In this project, we're essentially extending your shopping cart software onto Twitter—first, because it's easy to do, and second, because you will get extra marketing value out of every sale.

To start this project, write up a page on your site explaining how the sale works. On that page, ask your customers to shop your store as they normally would—right from your products through your shopping cart system and all the way through payment. They should complete their order entirely. Then, once the order is complete, ask them to send a tweet to all their friends containing:

- A #bogo hashtag
- Your username in the middle of the tweet (placing your username at the front of a tweet restricts who can see the message, and we want this to be über-public)
- A link to what they've purchased
- A link to what they want as their freebie
- Their order number

"Just bought great cider *http://jmcd.me/xqtYvm* (Order: 42532) from @farnumhillcider! Now my freebie: *http://jmcd.me/cider-freebie* #bogo"

You, as the shop owner, monitor your Twitter mentions and look for the #bogo tweets. For all the eligible entries, you simply need to include the extra freebie in their order and let the customer know that the freebie is on its way!

 Here's a quick caution. Always double-check that the tweet is original and not a retweet, and that the person's order number is legitimate. Retweets of these #bogo messages will confuse things. You don't want to send off free items willy-nilly.

Advanced Strategies

Other Items

If you're not comfortable giving so much away for free, you certainly don't have to use this method exactly. If you have a surplus of any particular item, you may want to offer that up as a freebie instead. The format of the customer's post-order tweet would have to change, of course.

"I just got this great cider *http://jmcd.me/xqtYvm* (Order:42532) from @farnumhillcider! Now gimme my free stickers!"

Twitter Integration

If you're savvy with your website, or you have an IT department at your disposal, you can make this process even easier for your customers by doing a little programming. Use Twitter's "Tweet This" link tool to create a standard "Tweet This" button on your shopping cart's receipt page. Then, in the button's options, replace the default "Tweet This" button text—which defaults to the page's title—with a promotional message, the customer's order number, your username, and any links you'd like in there.

With this integration complete, your site's receipt page will present the "Tweet This" button to all of your new customers—allowing them, in turn, to simply click the button to send out the preformatted tweet and collect their free gift. If you have the means, I recommend that you take the extra time to make this integration. You'll save your customers the trouble of creating their own tweets, and you will therefore receive more promotion.

CHAPTER 10

Discussion Groups

As I mentioned in my Introduction, the skeptics will tell you that it is impossible to have a worthwhile conversation in 140 characters or less. And, while I agree that at first glance this would appear to be true, the reality is that millions of Twitter fans find the platform an easy and effective way to have meaningful conversations.

One of the best examples of an organized discussion group I've seen on Twitter is run every Friday for one hour by Charlotte Abbot (@charabbott) and Kat Meyer (@katmeyer) under the hashtag #followreader. Follow the Reader is a blog that curates an ongoing discussion about, and exploration of, the book industry. Every week Charlotte and Kat invite their web community to gather on Twitter for an hour to speak, in real-time, about the issues of the day.

To participate in the organized chat, people need only to add #followreader to their tweets. All the folks watching that stream will then see the messages and respond using the same hashtag. In this way, folks can throw messages back and forth in rapid-fire at one time, publicly.

While Twitter wasn't intended originally to function as a chat room, it is surprisingly capable of being exactly that. I tend to see Twitter as the Internet's chat room—or the Internet's lobby. However, because the platform wasn't intended for this particular use, Twitter's own tools can sometimes make this style of interaction more difficult than it needs to be.

Independent software developers have recognized the shortcoming and offered up their own solutions to better organize this style of Twitter use. TweetChat, for example, allows people to filter all their incoming tweets down to only the ones containing a specific hashtag. Then, when you post a tweet through TweetChat, it automatically adds back in the hashtag you're following —thereby making your participating in the hashtag's discussion effortless.

Regularly scheduled discussion groups, should offer some value to your audience. Here are some ideas:

- An organized discussion of your topic or niche or industry
- A Q & A session with an expert from your company or your industry
- A weekly technical or strategy support chat for folks who would like advice
- A chance to ask your audience questions directly—perhaps to plan new products or improve existing ones

Whatever your topic, it is best to have an agenda and a time limit for each discussion. This way, you can promote the discussion easily during the week, keep folks on task when the conversation goes adrift, and can offer more than idle gabbing.

CHAPTER 11

Tweet Bombs

Tweet Bombs have been a part of Twitter since the very beginning. They are fun to do and can be very effective at grabbing a lot of quick attention, but I should caution you before I explain how to do it: Tweet Bombs need to be done carefully. Ill-fated or ill-spirited Tweet Bombs could damage your reputation with your audience, or label you as a spammer with Twitter. You'll see why.

A Tweet Bomb "is dropped" by a Twitter community on one of its unsuspecting members in the form of an avalanche of Twitter replies (or mentions). Hundreds, or thousands, of folks—at a coordinated moment—send tweets containing a particular user's username. The recipient's Reply (or Mention) stream is quickly inundated with messages. For folks who are used to seeing 3 or 4 mentions a day, seeing hundreds crashing down in a single minute can be startling. If done correctly, however, it is hilarious. Recipients of Tweet Bombs attest that the experience feels as though the whole Internet is looking straight at you.

To organize a Tweet Bomb, announce a time of the week to your followers when you'll be able to consistently drop a Tweet Bomb. By creating a regular schedule for your bombs, your audience will know when they should tune in to play along. When that time of the week rolls around, choose an unsuspecting member of your Twitter community as the recipient.

Be sure to choose that recipient carefully. When first starting out, it's best to pick someone you know to be easygoing or with whom you converse regularly. Once your audience is accustomed to seeing Tweet Bombs dropped, it will be safer to branch out a bit.

Send out a tweet alerting the rest of the community who it is that you've chosen, and the message that they should all send:

> "This week's #tweetbomb goes to @dpacheco! Message: "You look wonderful today." GO!"

Then, @dpacheco's Twitter stream fills up with messages from hundreds of people—mostly strangers. The messages look like this:

> "@dpacheco You look wonderful today."

And...it's totally weird for the recipient. As you can probably imagine, it's not hard to startle someone who doesn't know what a Tweet Bomb is with a message that might do more damage than good. "I see you..." is probably a bad one to start off with. Something like "Your hair looks nice today," might play better.

Beware of the dangers, use your better judgment, and you'll have a "blast." #groan

Advanced Strategies

Tweet Bomb Prizes

The only thing better than being the recipient of a Tweet Bomb is being the recipient of a Tweet Bomb that's full of freebies. If you're feeling flush and have got some goodies to give away, you can add a few freebies to your weekly Tweet Bomb. This will soften the blow of catching the sudden spotlight and will encourage people to come back and play every week for a chance to participate in showering someone with gifts and attention.

To give away something in your Tweet Bomb, be sure to include something about it—usually a link to a post explaining the prize—in your prewritten message:

> "This week's #tweetbomb goes to @dpacheco! Message: "Winner. Winner. Chicken dinner. *http://jmcd.me/AzZtCg*" GO!"

Then, when the recipient receives the message, they'll have a place to go to collect.

> @dpacheco Winner. Winner. Chicken dinner. *http://jmcd.me/AzZtCg*

CHAPTER 12

Web Scavenger Hunt

When I was a boy, every year on a chilly October morning, in preparation for hosting all the neighborhood kids at my birthday party, my parents would sneak around the yard of our brown saltbox suburban home stashing small plastic prizes and scribbled clues. The clues were scratched out in garbled cursive, so as to look old and mysterious—an effect created, I'm pretty sure, by my dad writing with his left hand. My parents were, of course, putting together a scavenger hunt.

The first clue was always placed under a frisbee in the center of the front yard. A group of us kids would bounce excitedly around the frisbee—mostly in anticipation of cake—until my dad called out from the front steps of the house, "GO!" We'd flip the frisbee, decipher the first clue, and scatter to the wind, very unstrategically scouring the yard for the next clue. We were off and running—our little heads occupied with the frenzy of the moment—and so my parents took the opportunity to go inside and ready the house for a dozen screaming eight-year-olds.

For reasons you can see, scavenger hunts have a soft spot in my heart. This project is modeled after my childhood scavenger hunts, but with a digital twist. To do correctly, this project will require some technical know-how, as you'll need to integrate a customized version of Twitter's "Tweet This" button into several pages of your site. If you're uncomfortable cutting and pasting JavaScript code into your website's HTML code, it's best to call on your IT department or hire a professional for the 5 or 10 minutes that the job would require.

In this scavenger hunt, you're going to lead your website visitors around your site using clues sent as tweets. The final location will contain a prize of some sort as a reward for your customers for sticking with you through the entire hunt. The pages you lead visitors to and through will be the pages on your site you'd most like people to visit—your products, services, sales, blog posts, etc. You'll see why in a moment.

You will need to create several "Tweet This" buttons using Twitter's creation tool. These will include:

- The first button, which will send the signal that someone is playing along
- The internal buttons, which send the promotional tweets of various site pages
- The final button, which reveals the prize to the winners

The first button will, when clicked, send a preformatted tweet that links back to the page on which it has been placed, includes a note about the scavenger hunt, references your username in the message, and contains the hashtag you've chosen for the scavenger hunt—#beaconscavengerhunt for example. It should end up looking like this:

> "Hunting for deals in the #beaconscavengerhunt! *http://jmcd.me/zl3RO5* via @beaconpressbks"

You'll then need to create a another "Tweet This" button for each internal page of your site that you'd like to include in your scavenger hunt. Each button will produce a tweet that contains your hashtag, your username, and a link to the page you're on. The message the button sends should be somewhat promotional for your company, ideally funny, and unique for each page. For example:

- For a product page:

    "Check out this video of the Cheese-Whipper 4000! *http://jmcd.me/wfUkXc* #beaconscavengerhunt"

- For a blog post:

    "Hilarious blog post about the mating rituals of sock puppets! *http://jmcd.me/zGzjSM* #beaconscavengerhunt"

- In general:

    "I'm doing the #beaconscavengerhunt today...while at work...of course. *http://jmcd.me/ws2U8B*"

Finally, you'll need to create the last "Tweet This" button, which will reveal to the participant that he has won the scavenger hunt. This final tweet will reveal the prize and provide a link.

Place the internal "Tweet This" buttons around your site on their appropriate pages first. These all need to be in place before you insert the final prize button and the starting button. You don't want people to jump into the race before the course is ready.

When all the internal page buttons are all in place and working, place the final prize button on the winning page, and then the first "Tweet This" button somewhere on your home page. Make sure you add some text above this first button so that it is clear to your visitors that this button is the starting point for your scavenger hunt.

After everything is set and tested, watch Twitter for the first message from a participant. When it pops up, you'll know you've got somebody playing.

Let's say that astronaut/physicist/humanitarian @daveburdick is the first to play:

> daveburdick tweets: "Hunting for deals in the #beaconscavengerhunt! *http://jmcd.me/zGzjSM* via @beaconpressbks"

Once you receive this message, reply to it privately with the clue that will lead @daveburdick to the next page in the hunt. Your participants must be following you in order for you to send them a direct message, so be sure to mention somewhere in your scavenger hunt rules or promotions that all participants must follow your account.

> "D daveburdick Hi! Welcome to the #beaconscavengerhunt. Your first clue: Purple Monkey Dishwasher"

When @daveburdick figures out the clue, he'll travel to the appropriate page —in this case a product page for the Simpsons DVD box set—and find another "Tweet This" button. Pressing that, he'll send out your preformatted tweet:

> daveburdick tweets: "I'm in love with this Simpsons DVD box set purple monkey dishwasher. *http://jmcd.me/yN9A1I* #beaconscavengerhunt"

When you see that he has found the page and tweeted its message, privately send him the next clue. Repeat this process until @daveburdick visits all the pages in your scavenger hunt, promotes each one to his followers, arrives at the final prize page, and tweets the final message:

> daveburdick tweets: "I outsmarted the *#beaconscavengerhunt*! I won this free hilarious t-shirt! *http://jmcd.me/AA1Fnr*"

The link contained in the last Twitter message should link to the product or prize won in the hunt. @daveburdick will click the link to see what he's won, and, in sending the tweet, he's promoted your scavenger hunt and hilarious t-shirt.

Ask @daveburdick for his mailing address and pop his freebie in the mail.

CHAPTER 13

Random Retweet

Here's a really simple way to keep your audience on its toes. This is a simple and quick project that I like to pepper it into a larger strategy when things get stale. This is the Random Retweet.

One of the best ways for your Twitter messages to reach the largest number of people is for your followers to retweet (or forward) your messages to their followers. The number of people following you directly—or, *your first order followers*—is puny when compared to cumulative number of people following your followers—or, your *second-order followers*. It is this audience you're hoping to reach. They are the audience that represents exponential growth.

There are two ways to go about earning retweets from your followers. The first is to send out excessively interesting, valuable, and insightful tweets—all the time. If you can do this, you'll be fine. The second way is to encourage retweets by dangling the odd carrot or two out in front of your would-be retweeters. Here's how.

Designate a few hours of every week—or even a full day, if you're feeling ambitious—during which you will run your "Random Retweet Riot" or "Retweet Happy Hour" or "Random Retweet Wednesdays" or whatever you choose to call your project.

Let your audience know that during the specified amount of time, every person to retweet one of your original messages will be eligible to win the contest. Then, at the end of the allotted time, pick a winner at random and thank everybody (individually) who retweeted one of your messages.

Advanced Strategies

There are plenty of curve balls you could throw into this Random Retweet project that might make it more interesting or challenging. Here are some quick variations you might want to give a try.

Nothing for Free

Why give away something for (virtually) nothing? Instead of giving away a freebie for just the click of a button, why not require that the randomly chosen winner first correctly answer a trivia question about your company, products, or services before declaring her the winner?

Third Time's a Charm

Don't choose a winner at random. Instead, declare the winner to be the third person to retweet any one tweet you send during that timeframe. This will encourage more retweets.

CHAPTER 14

A Picture is Worth 7.14 Tweets

If you've been shopping at any major retail site in the last year, you've probably noticed the "Share your Photos" links that sites have now integrated into product pages. Companies and merchants have taken a cue from the social media world and begun soliciting user-generated content for the sake of product promotion. The most popular form of which is the user-generated product shot.

Product shots take many forms: a laptop on a clean desk, a t-shirt in a bar, a stuffed bear on a ski lift, and so on. They can be funny or illustrative or exciting. But no matter style or tone of the photo, they all show products being used by happy customers out in the real world. This is a valuable community-building and marketing asset, and therefore, companies mine their customer communities for this photographic gold all the time.

You, however, can go a few steps beyond simply putting a request for product shots on your product pages. You have an active and engaged Twitter audience at your disposal, and having fun with product shots is a great way to build enthusiasm and community.

You may be asking, "Twitter for photos?! Isn't that Flickr?" And yes, sorta. Flickr is a great photo sharing site. But Twitter is the right place for this project, and I'll tell you why below. But before I get to that, it's useful to explain the process through which we came to have Twitter photo sharing.

When Twitter launched in 2006, it had no capacity for sharing photos. Nor could it use hashtags, or even send retweets. Originally, it was a barebones text broadcasting system. Its first design was—I imagine, intentionally—stripped of all the games and galleries and message boards and other puffery that crowds other popular social media platforms.

Twitter, instead, cut right to the core of modern human social interaction—the conversation—and, necessarily pithy conversations at that! Suddenly, people were forced to craft and refine their messages. This made communication more effective and more efficient. Gone were the pleasantries and conversational conventions that enable us all to write several paragraphs in an email without actually saying anything. Twitter requires us all to adhere to the lesson we learned from Strunk & White's *The Elements of Style:* omit unnecessary words.

Twitter today isn't much different, but it does have a few more tools and features. These additions weren't "designed" into the system. Twitter evolved. Most development projects—as many of you may know—begin with a development team planning out what they think would be "wicked cool," and then building and forcing that idea onto their users. Twitter approached the task differently. They, instead, waited to see how people interacted with the original barebones system, and then made their additions based on the needs of their users.

For example, when it became clear that Twitter users needed a better way to organize their conversations, hashtags were invented and suggested to the community by a user. Twitter integrated hashtag organization into their software only after people had widely adopted the practice.

Similarly, the ability to retweet messages wasn't in the original design either. Users took up the convention of prepending their messages with the letters "RT" (for ReTweet) and the username of the original author.

@bruceshaw tweets: "RT @jsmcdougall 'This conference should be in Boston next year! Also, I forgot my jacket in the bar...'"

Once the convention caught on, Twitter built the tools into their software.

The story is the same in the case of the recent addition of photo sharing to the Twitter platform. Third-party developers were the first to catch on to the need for a Twitter-specific photo-sharing utility. Services like TwitPic, yfrog.com, and img.ly quickly grew to be hugely popular. When Twitter saw that the users made heavy use of these third-party photo sharing services, they built photo sharing directly into Twitter to make the sharing of photos easier and more elegant for their users.

As a result of this responsive design process, Twitter is more in-tune with the human communication process than many other social platforms. Because it grew naturally, it feels more natural to users, and allows them—in turn—to *be* more natural while communicating with others. There is no shoehorn into which you must squeeze your life. You simply communicate, and the tools you need are at hand.

This makes Twitter the perfect platform through which to request photos from your audience. They no longer need to fiddle and futz with other websites to send you photos (though they certainly *can* if they choose).

There are several variations of this project. You can keep things simple by asking that people just post their product shots, or you can run a contest and give away a prize for the "best" or "funniest" or "most bizarre" product shots. Or, you can go all out and give away multiple prizes for every 5th or 10th or 30th person to send in a photo.

No matter how you choose to run the project, begin with a simple tweet announcing the contest and linking people to a blog post detailing the rules. Here are some rules I recommend:

- No nudity. Must be G-rated.
- A product from the company/store must be prominently displayed in the photograph.
- Must have permission from everyone depicted in the photo to post the photo publicly online.
- Once you submit the photo to our contest, you grant us the rights to use the photo for our own promotional campaigns.
- All photo entries must be submitted to us through Twitter, in a tweet containing a link to the photo; a link to the page on our website for the product in the photo; our username "@johnnyseeds"; and the contest hashtag #johnnyseedsphotos.

As people begin to upload and tweet photos to you, retweet them out to your own audience with some commentary on each photo. This will encourage your followers to grab their mobile phones and start snapping some quick shots of their own. Your goal is to start the snowball rolling with the first few entries. The positive feedback loop is your friend.

Download the images to your computer for use later. They will be useful in promotions, on your product pages, and on your other social media outlets.

This contest will produce a lot of attention for you on Twitter—people looooove looking at goofy pictures—and, at the end of the project, you will have a collection of valuable photos of happy customers using your products in the real world—and permission to use the photos as you see fit!

When all the images are in, put together a blog post with all the photos in a gallery. Thank the participants and list the prizes you've given away, if any.

CHAPTER 15

The Star in the Crowd

I used to dream of being a rock star. My older brother was a musician and I wanted to tour the country rocking out every night and relaxing every day. I dreamed of throwing giant concerts in packed stadiums with tens of thousands of people waiting to hear me play.

My thought was that I'd put on a hat and glasses and mill about in the crowd before the show. Moving through the crowds—disguised and sheepish —I would listen in on what people were talking about, see who was in the crowd, and get a feel for what it was like to be in the audience. If I was ever discovered, I thought, I'd hand out some backstage passes and all would be fine.

Finally, in fifth grade, when it came time for me to choose an instrument to play in the student band, I told my mother I would be learning the drums. She told me I would be learning the violin. And so it was. No concerts. No crowd. But twenty years later I can still bang out a nasty "Mary Had A Little Lamb" on the ol' horsehair.

This project is a variation of my childhood "rockstar in the crowd" idea. It's a fun project to do at popular public spaces such as sporting events, conferences, or public concerts. The point of this project is not to garner huge public attention or drive people to your website. The point, instead, is to quietly reward and thank your followers for their attention by seeking them out and giving them some sort of gift or gift certificate.

Here are a couple ways it could work.

Let's pretend for a moment that you're the owner of a chain of high-quality gelato shops stretching from Maine to D.C., called Morano Gelato. Your username is @moranogelato. Your shops offer WiFi, couches, and a "cool" atmosphere. People often take advantage of your hospitality by sitting and lounging while getting some work done.

To kick things off, walk into any of your crowded gelato shops and send out a tweet to all your followers.

> @moranogelato: "At the Boylston Street Morano Gelato. If you're in here too, meet me at the fireplace to win a free year of coffee."

If someone shows up, you've got a winner! If no one does, your audience will be looking for you the next time they stop in.

If you would like to offer this sort of reward to your followers more often than it is possible for you to do on your own, you can delegate the contest responsibilities to the managers at each of your locations. Boloco (@boloco), for example, has a Twitter account set up for each of its locations, all of which could give away freebies to people inside the restaurant every month. This would incentivize repeat customers, create a fun atmosphere, build a Twitter following, and encourage rapid word-of-mouth "get-your-butt-down-here" marketing.

I promise that the Twitter-addicted winner of the giveaway will immediately tell all their followers what just happened. You'll probably get a photo too! #FTW

OK, so you don't own restaurants. Neither do I. Let's say you've got a sporting goods store in Burlington, Vermont called the Outdoor Gear Exchange. Your username is @gearxcom. The next time you take in a game at UVM, take along a stack of gift certificates. At halftime, when everybody is loading up on hot dogs and beer, stand beside the escalators and send a tweet:

> @gearxcom: "At the UVM game in front of exit 5. Any followers here? Find me for $50 off!"

When people show up, take a photo, send a tweet, and pass out a gift certificate.

Finally, let's say you're an average Joe attending a standard industry conference and want to drum up some followers for your Twitter account: @HCPDishes. Not everyone at the conference will know you and most won't be following you. If you send a tweet, chances are that no one will see it. So, to gain some exposure for your tweet, piggy-back on the conference's hashtag. In this case, you'll need to send two tweets:

@HCPDishes: "At the #moocon conference. Follow us to learn how to win a free stack of cookbooks!"

Then, once you see that you've got people at the #moocon conference following you, and everyone is milling about at a lunch break, send out your next tweet:

@HCPDishes: "I'm standing at the conference cheese table. First one to find me wins the books!"

Notice that there is no hashtag in your second tweet. You don't want to share that message with everybody at the conference—only those who took the time and interest to follow you. When a person shows up to claim the stack of books, shove the gentleman into the softened brie and run off with the prize yourself. It's win-win.

CHAPTER 16

Digital Hide & Seek

Cover your eyes. Count to ten. Call out "Ready or not! Here I come!", and run frantically around the house searching for all the children you will need to rescue from your cabinets and laundry baskets. It's a silly and familiar game, but it passes the time with laughter and surprises.

This project is the same thing...only you play it online and instead hearing the magic of a child's laughter, you'll be reading the underwhelming acronym, "LOL." But while this version of the game pales in comparison to playing it with real-live kids, it does do a good job of getting lots of people scouring through your online store hunting for something you've hidden...but instead finding amazing deals along the way! #groan

To get this project started, find a goofy photo that, in some way, relates to your company. If you run a pizza shop, it could be an animated GIF of a dancing pizza. If you run a kennel, it could be a photo of a puppy napping upside-down. If you work in applied logistics...take a picture of yourself making a funny face. The world has no funny photos of applied logistics. Let's say, for the sake of example, that you run a motorcycle shop in Massachusetts called Mohawk Cycle Sales.

Comb through your website searching for a funny place to insert the image. You could replace a product image with the funny photo, or put it in at the bottom of a blog post, or replace a staff photo on your biographies page. The photo should be hidden from plain view (that is, hidden from the casual visitor's über-fast scanning), but it should appear obviously out-of-place when found. People who find the photo and aren't playing will chuckle and assume that you're a company with a sense of humor—unless, of course, you work in applied logistics.

Once you've placed the photo, send out a tweet stating the simple rules and displaying the photo you've hidden. (Don't link to the page on which you've hidden the image. Instead, upload the image to Twitter or TwitPic and send it out separately.)

> "I've hidden this image *http://jmcd.me/x0GjNv* on our site. Be the first to tweet the page it's on and win $50 off! GO! *http://www.greenmountain bikes.com* RT!"

Send this tweet every hour or so until someone wins. Of course, you can vary the message from tweet-to-tweet so that people don't get annoyed with your promotion of it. Also, it's often a good idea to ask people to retweet your messages to their friends by inserting the suggestion "RT?" at the end of your message. Simply by planting the idea to hit the retweet button in your message, your tweets will get retweeted more often.

People will flow into your website and hunt for the hidden image. If you subscribe to a real-time traffic tracking service like ChartBeat (*http://chartbeat .com*), you can watch in real-time as people jump from page to page, scroll down, and continue on. It's thrilling to watch, and quite addictive. Bring popcorn.

For web masters and marketers who spend hours upon hours and tens of thousands of dollars trying to lure people into a website with Google ads and Facebook ads and Blogads and so on, it's thrilling to sit back and watch people enter your site and comb through it—all for the price of several tweets and a small gift certificate. Creativity is valuable to your company.

If you are watching your traffic on ChartBeat, then you'll likely know when a person finds the image before he does. You'll be able to see when he lands on the particular page, and when he scrolls down far enough to find it. If he moves on, he's scanned too quickly. If he finds it, he'll send out the winning tweet.

> "@mohawkcycle I've found it! It's here! *http://www.mohawkcycles.com/ products/rock-hopper*"

Write up the gift certificate—or, if your e-commerce platform allows it, create the discount code—and send it off to the winner.

Repeat as necessary.

CHAPTER 17

Smile. You're on Camera.

Two of the most common forms of contests online are photo contests and video contests. Even before the Internet made the creation and sharing of multimedia easy, companies were exchanging cash and prizes for compelling multimedia involving their products. Obviously, the Internet and the proliferation of cheap, high-quality cameras have only made this process easier. Now, nearly anyone can create multimedia content if properly compelled to do so. For little work and not too much expense, this style of project will help you create a social media marketing war chest of user-submitted content.

Do some research and strategic planning before striking out on this project. Come up with a contest that will target and engage your ideal customers. You may need to experiment a bit before you find an approach that strikes a chord, but grant yourself—or your employees—the flexibility to do so. Don't assume that you've got it right (or that you have been as successful as is possible) in your first attempt. There are many ways to approach this project, and the approach you take should account for your audience, your products, your company, your branding, and your personality.

For example, if you're Shelf Stackerz—a new company with a brilliant new shelf-organization system, and you haven't sold many of your systems yet, it would be difficult for you to successfully solicit product testimonials from your audience simply because most people in your audience won't yet have your systems organizing their shelves. Therefore, your goal with this contest isn't primarily product promotion, but product introduction.

Instead of running a contest based on product testimonials, run a contest that's instead based on the larger theme of organization. You'll find many more organizationally obsessed folks than you will already-satisfied customers.

- An "Everything In Its Place" photo contest
- A "How Well Do You Organize?" video contest
- A "Yeah, But..Where Do I Park the Car?" garage disaster photo contest
- An "I Should Probably Be On Hoarders" house disaster video contest

All of these contests target folks who love organization and would want your products...or folks who *need* organization, and need your products.

If your company has been around a while and you've got a healthy and happy customer base, you'll have an easier time soliciting product testimonials. Let's say you're Volkl, a major ski manufacturer. You have the advantages of worldwide recognition, an active customer base, and a mostly young audience.

You could set up your contest to solicit barebones customer product testimonials:

> The "Tell Us What Model of Ski You Have and Why You Like Them" Video Contest

This approach will absolutely produce a bunch of videos that will be great for your product pages, but they'll also sound like a bunch of 8th grade book reports—not very compelling when used as marketing materials. Instead, leverage the advantages you have in your audience and ask your customers to produce something a bit more engaging:

> The "Show Us Where You Take Your Volkls" Photo & Video Contest

This approach will produce videos and photos that have been taken outside —in majestic landscapes—while people are enjoying your skis. This user-generated content will be social media marketing gold for you. People will love to see it and love to share it.

There are many tools your audience can use to create and share their photos and videos. In your initial write-up about the contest, give people some recommendations as to which tools they could use to deliver their content to you. This will make organization of the content much easier for you, and the method of collection will determine whether or not you will have access to the content after the contest is over.

Collect photos through any popular sharing service—Flickr, Twitter, TwitPic, etc. Collecting images via email is possible, but it is not a public process, and you will therefore sacrifice some promotional value.

The method you use to collect videos will depend on how long you'd like to have access to the submitted content. Many video contests only ask that the user submit their video to a popular video hosting platform like Vimeo or YouTube or Flickr. This is a perfectly acceptable method for collection as it makes the videos public, plunks them down in a sea of millions of users, and allows you to embed them on your own website. The downside of this approach is that you will not—in most cases—have access to the raw video file. If the user decides to take that video offline for any reason, you will no longer be able to use it in your promotions. Therefore, I recommend that you collect the raw video files directly through a "large file transfer" service such as We-Transfer.com or YouSendIt.com. Once you have the raw video files in your possession, you can upload the files to any video service of your choice, embed the videos in your own site, and keep the files for later use.

Finally, knowing how to target your contest is vitally important if you're going to reach the maximum number of ideal customers. Many of your ideal customers do not follow you on Twitter, and most do not know you exist at all. Therefore, sending a tweet out to your followers with no consideration for the larger audience will only reach a fraction of the people you need. There are other things you must do.

Hashtags are the key to growth on Twitter. When you include a hashtag in your message, you're exposing that message to everybody who is following that topic's hashtag. So, while the ski buffs and bunnies you're targeting may not be following @volkl, they are likely to be following the #skiing and #backcountryskiing and #slalom hashtags. Use your Twitter client's search feature—or *http://search.twitter.com*—to investigate the various hashtags in your niche and find the ones that have the most activity. Then, use those hashtags in your post to target the non-followers who are interested in that topic.

Another great targeting tactic is to enlist the help of bigger fish. So, let's say you're Shelf Stackerz and you've only got a few hundred people following you. Obviously, your ideal audience is much larger than a few hundred people. While you may not yet have everybody in your ideal audience following you, somebody does. Seek out that larger Twitter account in your niche and introduce yourself. Investigate whether the largest home/style/organization blogs and magazines have Twitter accounts and followings. Once you start your contest, ask them for help promoting it. A simple and friendly retweet can put your contest in front of tens of thousands of ideal customers—but you've got to do the work of finding and targeting the folks with those audiences.

There are countless ways to judge a photo or video contest. Many contest operators simply pick their favorite. I'll leave it to you to decide how to determine the winner. My only caution is to never play favorites. People will know when you pick your girlfriend's video, and you don't want to deal with the fallout from that. Have fun!

CHAPTER 18

Half-Off Hangman

I've made no secret of my distaste for coupon campaigns on Twitter, and it is with some reluctance
that I include a coupon code project in this book.
My distaste stems from the sheer laziness of the
general practice. It take no effort or creativity to
simply tweet out coupon or discount codes. People
do not join Twitter for discounts! People join Twitter for engaging interactions with the people they
know and meet. Coupon campaigns tend not to be
engaging nor interactive.

And yet, Twitter coupon campaigns happen so often that people tend to come
to think of Twitter marketing as nothing more than sending out coupon codes
—and then, the followers who aren't interested in marketing begin to regard
these tweets as *spam*. It's "bad news bears."

Remember, there's only one way to get unfollowed on Twitter, and that's by
annoying your audience. Even being silent is better than being annoying, and
repeatedly tweeting out coupon codes runs the risk of annoying your followers.
Approach with caution.

If used correctly, coupon or discount codes can be useful in engaging your
audience—but only when used within the context of a more interesting project
or campaign. Therefore, I've designed the following project to make use of
coupon codes in a way that is both engaging and interactive. Hopefully, this
will help reverse the trend I'm seeing of companies dumping this sort of tweet
on us all:

> "NOW until Christmas! 10% off all our slacks and fedoras! Use this code
> at checkout: TWIT12 *http://jmcd.me/zaP4Vl*"

Puke.

...so here's Half-Off Hangman!

Modern e-commerce platforms allow retailers and e-tailers and Shopifiers (*http://www.shopify.com*) and FoxyShoppers (*http://www.foxyshop.com*) and even eBayers (*http://www...*you know this one) to create discount codes. Sometimes, these are a short pseudo-phrase defined by the shopkeeper: XMAS2012, or TWIT, or DEAL1. Sometimes, these are a series of randomly generated characters—either by machine or by the shopkeeper: Rf7Dh, 333DsUy, and so on.

As I said in my rant above, too many shopkeepers just shout these out to their audiences. I prefer to use these odd little series of characters to first engage the audience in a game before I unleash the code to the world. This achieves two things: first, it draws more attention to the discount, and therefore more people will ultimately use it; and second, it makes following you fun.

Start this project by creating the discount code in your e-commerce software. For the sake of example, let's say that you are a cookbook publisher and you're ramping up your holiday promotion of baking books. Let's also say that you have the ability to create the code yourself and you choose the phase: vanillaextract. This is now your discount code and anyone who uses it during checkout gets 50% off your baking books.

Send out a few tweets introducing the game, the prize, the number of characters, the number of guesses they're allowed to get wrong, and the hashtag.

> @HCPDishes tweets: "We're playing #halfoffhangman for 50% off our baking books. Guess, but don't get more than 6 wrong! Phrase to follow..."
> @HCPDishes tweets: "The #halfoffhangman phrase for 50% off our baking books: _ _ _ _ _ _ _ _ _ _ _ _ _ _ Go!"

People will respond to you with their letters and guesses.

> @_applegang_ tweets: "@HCPDishes a! #halfoffhangman"
> @pmcd tweets: "@HCPDishes Is there an e? #halfoffhangman"
> @shaytotten tweets: "@HCPDishes What about a q? #halfoffhangman"

And as the letters come in, fill in the letters for people.

> @HCPDishes tweets: ".@_applegang_ got the a's! _ a _ _ _ _ a _ _ _ _ a _ _! Wrong: 0/6 #halfoffhangman"
> @HCPDishes tweets ".@pmcd got some e's... _ a _ _ _ _ a e _ _ _ a _ _! Wrong: 0/6 #halfoffhangman"
> @HCPDishes tweets "I'm sorry @shaytotten! No q's. Keep guessing so that the discount code is revealed! Wrong: 1/6 #halfoffhangman"

Notice that I've added a period before the usernames of the people I'm replying to (.@pmcd). Twitter limits the exposure of your tweets based on what you place at the front of your message. If you put a username at the front of your message, the tweet is shown only to that user and is left out of the general stream. I add the period before the username to make sure the tweet is as public as possible.

Keep track of how many people guess incorrectly and stop the project if people exceed the limit you've set. I know it seems counterproductive to withhold the discount code from the people you want to use it, but without risk, this game is no fun. And fun will do more marketing work for you than the discount ever could.

When all the letters have been revealed or someone has guessed the phrase—in this case, we'll assume it was astronaut/physicist/humanitarian @daveburdick again:

> @daveburdick tweets: "@HCPDishes I know! It's vanillaextract! #winning #halfoffhangman"

At that point, reveal the right answer and invite everybody to celebrate the win by using the code for 50% off your baking books.

> #HCPDishes tweets: "Congrats @daveburdick! Now everybody can use the code for 50% off anything here: *http://jmcd.me/xM9mft* #half-offhangman"

This is a fun way to tease your audience with the discount, prolong the suspense, and encourage positive engagement with your company. Plus, isn't it way more fun that just blurting it out?!

CHAPTER 19

Topic Quotes

Every business has a niche—or several niches—in which it operates. Every niche has its heroes. Every hero has his or her quotes—which usually boil down to 140 characters or fewer. See where I'm going with this?

Sharing quotes from the heavy-hitters within your niche is a great engagement project for the slower days in your marketing calendar. This project won't drive traffic or sales, but it will keep your audience active and it will pitch you and your company as a leader in the niche.

Running this project is dirt simple. Pick your favorite saying or quote from someone in your niche and send it out with an appropriate hashtag. After you send out the first quote, invite others to contribute their own.

> @catalystwebwks tweets: "Being the richest man in the cemetery never mattered to me. - Steve Jobs #inspiringtechquotes"
> @triumphofficial tweets: "I'm not sure whether I'm an actor who races or a racer who acts. - Steve McQueen #greatracequotes"
> @phoenixsuns tweets: "What happened in the past is just that, the past. Champion or not. - Steve Nash #sportsquotes"

As you're the one launching the project, you have the freedom to determine the theme of the quotes you'd like to collect and share. You can ask for funny quotes, inspirational quotes, insightful quotes, or even topic-based quotes. For example, if London Fog (@londonfogbrand)—the famous raincoat company—wanted to start up this project, they could ask for "rain quotes for our raincoats."

@londonfogbrand tweets: "A crown is merely a hat that lets the rain in. - Frederick the Great #RainQuotesForRainCoats"

And the audience would respond.

@makenna_goodman tweets: "Haha! 'I think fish is nice, but then I think rain is wet, so who am I to judge. - Douglas Adams' #RainQuotesForRainCoats"

If quotes are hard to come by for your niche—as would be if you work in applied logistics—you can expand your project from attributable quotes to include general sayings and phrases as well.

@britb tweets: "@londonfog Rain, Rain, Go Away. #LondonFogRainQuotes"

Collect up all your favorite submissions so that you can write up a blog post about the project later on. Be sure to retweet your favorites.

CHAPTER 20

Twitter Trivia

Yes, I refuse to call the Twitter trivia project, "Twivia." I hope you appreciate that.

Despite what its Latin definition might lead you to believe, trivia is not trivial. Trivia questions have created game show empires, reinvented the American board game, and breathed new life back into Wednesday nights at your local bar. Now, you can make use of our cultural fascination with trivia to light a fire underneath your Twitter audience. Engage while you educate. Pontificate while you promote.

As with all of the projects in this book, the concept is simple, and there are many ways to approach the task. You will need to define a goal for your trivia project before you get started. Your goals will determine not only your questions, but how you run the game.

First, decide if you'd like to ask questions based on your niche, your company, or your products.

If you're a content-producing company like a news organization, a book publisher, a magazine, or a blog, you will probably want to ask trivia questions based on your niche.

You could, of course, ask people questions about your products, but "What is the ISBN for "Rainwater Harvesting, Volume 1?" isn't very compelling. However, "Which is the only US state to make rainwater harvesting illegal?" has more teeth to it. People will want to know. "Collecting rain? In a bucket? Illegal?!"

Likewise, if your topic is gardening, and your audience is devoted to and familiar with gardening, feel free to fire away any gardening trivia questions you have:

@chelseagreen tweets: "Who pioneered four-season farming in the frozen northeast? #gardeningtrivia *http://jmcd.me/y1GNpR*"

News organizations could ask questions about the week's headlines, what happened on this date in history, or the odd breakfast habits of today's political leaders. If you feel inclined to provide your audience with a hint, you could include a link to where the answer can be found on your site:

@vprnet tweets: "What strange food does Vladimir Putin eat for breakfast? #topstorytrivia *http://jmcd.me/y1ko79*"

If you're a well-known manufacturer of consumer products—oh, let's say... Apple—you could use your own products as your topic for trivia. (Author's note: Apple isn't on Twitter yet. I've made up a username.)

@apple tweets: "What was the name of the first Apple tablet? Hint: Not iPad. *http://apple.com/history* #appletrivia"

The key here is, of course, that people have to care. I'm sorry to say it, but if you're not Apple and don't have rockstar products, this is harder to do:

@appliedlogistics tweets: "In what year did we introduce the JM-1020 to the Southeast Asian market? *http://jmcd.me/wfEsq9* #snoozetrivia"

This just won't fly.

Finally, if you've got a long and storied company history, dig into your own record books to find some interesting trivia questions. You don't have to be famous in this case—just interesting:

@toyota tweets: "Who invented and holds the patent for those QR codes you're seeing everywhere? #toyotatrivia *http://jmcd.me/zLNb73*"

Author's note: Toyota does.

Once you've decided how you're going to approach this project, come up with a list of 5 or 10 questions (and links if you want to include them) to tweet out during the course of a day.

If anyone in your audience is able to answer all your questions correctly, reward that person with a prize or praise—as you see fit. Be sure, as always, to thank everybody for playing along.

CHAPTER 21

Twitter Telephone

Twitter is always evolving. Users are constantly in-
venting new ways to organize and manage their
messages. One of the newest conventions to catch
on is the "MT" or Modified Tweet. This is similar
to an "RT" or ReTweet, except instead of quoting
a tweet exactly, the sender modifies the original
message slightly—while (hopefully) retaining the
original meaning—before sending it.

Tweet This...

> Original Tweet by @timoreilly: "I finally fig-
> ured out the future of profitable publishing.
> I've written all the secrets here: *http://jmcd.me/
> zZJ1IO*"

> Retweet: "RT @timoreilly: I finally figured out the future of profitable
> publishing. I've written the secrets here *http://jmcd.me/zZJ1IO*"

> Modified Tweet: "MT @timoreilly 'I figured out the future of publishing.'
> Well it's about time! We've all been waiting."

This particular project takes the MT concept, and intensifies it for fun and
engagement. This is a game of Twitter Telephone. It won't drive traffic. Nor
will it drive sales. But if you're looking for something to remind people you're
around and put some pep into your Twitter audience on a sleepy afternoon,
this game is quick, fun, and easy.

The concept is simple. Write a message or phrase and pass it on to ONE person
by placing that user's username at the beginning of your tweet. Add in the
game's hashtag (#tt) and ask the recipient of the tweet to change one word of
the message and pass it on to another person.

You tweet: "@leftlane 'These pretzels are making me thirsty.' #tt #twittertelephone #changethephraseandpassiton"

@leftlane tweets: "@kalenski 'These pretzels are making me confused.' #tt #twittertelephone #changethephraseandpassiton"

@kalenski tweets: "@charabbott 'These pantsuits are making me confused.' #tt #twittertelephone #changethephraseandpassiton"

Watch the hashtag stream to see the message mutate over time. My hope is that the game catches on and that the #tt hashtag—for Twitter Telephone— will be recognizable enough to suffice as both an indicator of the game and directions for how to play. As you can see, the #twittertelephone and #changethephraseandpassiton tags eat up a lot of valuable real estate. Unfortunately, they're helpful when introducing the game to your audience. If your phrase is so long that it makes adding these tags impossible, you could write up a blog post explaining the game and how it works, and then link to it in every tweet.

You tweet: "@leftlane 'These pretzels are making me thirsty.' #tt *http:// jmcd.me/zQTSWk*"

@leftlane tweets: "@kalenski 'These pretzels are making me confused.' #tt *http://jmcd.me/zOLIyO*"

And so on.

If you'd like to incentivize the game a bit, you could offer prizes or gift certificates to the participants. You certainly don't want or need to offer a prize to everyone who plays, but you might do well to offer every 10th, 20th, or 100th person who forwards the message a little something—even if it's as simple as a tweet to your massive audience promoting the participant's website or Twitter account.

One final note: As this game catches on, people will be inclined to shorten the name of the game from Twitter Telephone to simply, "Twelephone." If you encounter this transformation, please beat the offending person with your shoe. You have my permission. I invented it.

Purple monkey dishwasher.

CHAPTER 22

Where In The World Is...?

For any business with an investment in a particular area—whether that's a state, city, or neighborhood —it's important for people in that area feel as though that company is part of the community— and that you, as the business owner or manager, do and feel the same things that they do and feel.

We've entered a time when consumers are demanding more transparency from the businesses and organizations with which they choose to interact. The rise of social media only contributes to —and encourages—the public's desire to meet the "man behind the curtain." We want to spend our money with people who can be held accountable, and who care as much about preserving and improving our communities as we do.

This project is designed to help you build a connection with your audience by promoting your investment in the area and community in which you do business. This project should not be used to create the *illusion* that you care about your community. You don't want to put one over on your audience. So if you don't care, move on. But, I'm sure you do care. You're a good person. I like you.

This project is inspired by the old television show and early-PC computer game, "Where in the World is Carmen Sandiego?" And yes, they spelled it "Sandiego." The game was targeted to kids and showed photos of world landmarks. The kids then guessed the country or city in which Carmen was hiding out.

In our version of the game, you take to the streets of your area armed with some sort of company paraphernalia (a t-shirt, a button, a van, etc.), a mobile camera, and a notepad. As you pass local landmarks, jump out and snap a photo of your t-shirt, button, or van out in front of the landmark. Also, jot down some trivia-like notes or riddles that you can use to ask your audience later.

Don't limit yourself to historical landmarks. Get photos of popular local hangouts, notorious traffic snarls, places of local legend, familiar graffiti, and anything else the local population would immediately recognize and appreciate.

Depending on the size of your area, this project may take significant time. If you run a pizza delivery service, a messenger, or any other sort of business with drivers, pass out some t-shirts and cameras to the crew and ask them to snap some shots. If your area is limited to a few city blocks, you could compile a good list of notes and all your photographs in a fun afternoon.

Once you've collected your photos and notes, start putting together your questions, riddles, or clues. You don't necessarily need to pair photos and clues, but it's fun if you do.

When everything is compiled, start sending out your tweets.

> @bolocohanover tweets: "It's time to play #whereintheworld! I'm going to send out 10 clues for 10 locations. Guess them all to win! *http://jmcd.me/yeODLX*"
> @bolocohanover tweets: "Your 1st #whereintheworld clue: *http://jmcd.me/xnJ01u*"
> @bolocohanover tweets: "Your 2nd #whereintheworld clue: I'm always full, and yet you always try anyway. Where am I?"

Your local followers will call out:

> @jsmcdougall tweets: "@bolocohanover The fire tower in Norwich! #whereintheworld"
> @jsmcdougall tweets: "@bolocohanover The parking lot behind Boloco Hanover! #whereintheworld"

The first person to guess all 10 locations correctly wins the prize—whatever that may be. Your local audience will appreciate your dedication and familiarity with the local area. If you're not familiar with your local area, and would like to give this project a go anyway, grab one of your local employees who is familiar with the area and let him or her ride shotgun. Your followers will thank you for it.

Good luck!

CHAPTER 23

I Feel So Close To You Right Now

One feature of Twitter we haven't much explored in this book is Twitter's "location" function. For those of you who are unfamiliar with this feature, I'll explain.

Big Brother never had it so easy. We, as a culture, have surrendered any privacy we had left for the fun of telling our friends and followers exactly where we are in every moment. We are our own paparazzi. The mobile phones in our pockets fire off public reports whenever we walk into our favorite coffee shop, bookstore, or house of ill-repute. (Just kidding! We turn off our phones before *that* happens.)

Location-based social platforms like FourSquare have turned this constant surveillance into a flashy game for us to play. And you may not know about it because they don't promote it much, but Twitter also has integrated its own mobile location-tracking ability. You can, if you wish, attach your current location to your current tweet. You can also turn this feature off if you want to go about your day privately—but what fun would that be? Google's satellites are watching us move about anyway, so let's have fun with it, shall we?! #rant

This project uses Twitter's location feature to keep your audience on its toes. I call this the "I feel so close to you right now" project. The premise is similar to the "Star in the Crowd" project, in that you're out in the real world looking for other followers in the real world—but instead of meeting your followers face-to-face, you're searching in a much larger geographic area, making face-to-face interaction impossible.

To get started, send out a tweet in the morning announcing that at a designated time during the day, you'll be sending out a request for your followers to tweet their locations. The follower who tweets in reply from the location closest to you will win the designated prize. In order to be eligible, the participants' tweets must be tagged with the participant's location (as opposed to simply stated in the tweet), must include the contest hashtag, and must be in reply to your call for locations.

> @clairesvt tweets: "Today at 3pm EST, we'll be asking for your location. If you're the one closest to us, you will win free lunch! #ifeelsoclosetoyourightnow"

Then, at 3 p.m.:

> @clairesvt tweets: "It's 3pm! Attach your location to your tweet and let us know where you are! The closest one wins! #ifeelsoclosetoyourightnow"
>
> @justin_willman tweets: "This game is magical! And I'm here!" (Location: Barre, VT)
>
> @photomatt tweets: "Word! Pressed the location button. Here I am!" (Location: Boston, MA)
>
> @simonstl tweets: "This game is the bees knees. I hope I'm closest." (Location: Burlington, VT)

As the tweets come rolling in, enter the usernames of the tweeters into a tweet-mapping service such as MyTweetMap.com (*http://mytweetmap.com*). You, and your participants, will be able to see who is tweeting from where.

After all the tweeting slows down, tweet a link to the map you've created, and declare the person with the closest pin to your location the winner.

The great thing about this project is that as long as someone plays, someone wins. Your geographic in this project is planet Earth. So if you're in Atlanta, and someone in Hong Kong is the only person to play—you're mailing a prize to Hong Kong!

More importantly, you're giving your location to everyone you're following. If you're at the head of a popular Twitter account, you're somewhat of a celebrity in many people's eyes—and by giving out your location, you're placing yourself in the world in which your followers travel. You come down to their level in their eyes, and they will appreciate that from you. Remember, social media is often most effective when you're giving people a peek behind the curtain—letting people know you're human—and this project does that quite effectively.

CHAPTER 24

I've Got The Golden Ticket!

You've seen the dance. You've heard the song. You can probably picture most of the scene right now. It might be the famous fictional contest ever created. The excitement that erupts when Charlie and his grandfather find the fifth golden ticket in Willy Wonka's chocolate bar is now embedded in the collective American memory. It's a great moment in film, and it can be a great moment for you as well. This project aims to recreate that excitement —at least in a small way—for you and your own customers.

Tweet This...

If you've got a business that ships products to customers, wholesalers, or retailers, you can make this project work for you. If you've got a restaurant that wraps food in any way before serving it, this project could work for you. And, if you've got a retail shop, and can slip tickets in your customers' bags, this project could work for you. If you're a bookstore and can slip a golden bookmark into your customers' books, this project could work for you. If you're creative and think through your customer interaction process, I bet you can find a way to slip a ticket in there somewhere.

This project requires a fair amount of preparation and promotion, so, if you're thinking you're going to give this one a shot, be sure to set aside enough time and resources to pull it off successfully.

The first step is to get excited! You get to play the role of Willy Wonka! Just... without the chocolate waterfall, I'm afraid. If you get excited about the project and the fact that you get to do it at work, then you will have an easier time convincing your customers to get excited about the prospect of winning the contest.

Begin by planning an appropriate time to conduct this project. You will spend a lot of time promoting the contest, so make sure you choose a time where the extra work and attention will pay off most effectively—the run up to the holidays, leading up to a summer sales event, or piggybacking on another promotional campaign you're doing. I recommend running the contest for at least a month.

Once you've chosen your time slot, you will need to design your tickets. You will need winning tickets and losing tickets. Your five winning tickets do not have to be gold. If...oh, I don't know...paper better fits your color scheme and budget, use paper. Even be daring and use blue if it suits you and your branding. Gold-colored paper is a good option, however, if you would like to capitalize on your audience's familiarity with Willy Wonka's contest.

The losing tickets should say something like this:

> "I'm sorry, you didn't win this time. But thanks for playing in the Boulder Book Store Golden Ticket contest. To learn more, visit *http://www.boulderbookstore.com/golden-ticket/*"

The winning ticket, however, should explode with excitement...and instructions:

> "You've found the 2nd Golden Ticket! Congratulations! You've won our grand prize! To claim your prize, simply tweet the following phrase, exactly as it appears here: 'I've found the 2nd Golden Ticket from @boulderbooks! I've won the grand prize! -whizbang- *http://jmcd.me/x4YLS5* #goldenticket'. Then, tweet a photo of the ticket and share it with all your followers! Congrats!"

The message on the Golden Ticket does a few things. First, it congratulates the winner and let's her know what she's won. Second, it provides instructions on what to do next. Third, it includes the text of a tweet which contains your username, a promotional message, the number of the ticket found, a link to the contest rules, and a unique security phrase "-whizbang-", which lets you know the ticket is authentic. The security phrase should be different on each ticket. Finally, the ticket asks the recipient to send a photo of the ticket out to Twitter. This will provide you with some extra validation that the ticket is what you created, and will give you a little more promotion.

If you're totally paranoid (or careful), scribble something unique on each winning ticket before you send it out. Check each photographed ticket for that same scribble.

Once you've got all the tickets designed, written, and printed, it's time to begin promoting the contest.

Start by writing up a blog post announcing the contest and detailing the rules. I recommend putting together a video explaining how the contest works and posting it to all your social media accounts—Facebook, Tumblr, LinkedIn, Vimeo, etc. Also, write up an email newsletter promoting the contest and linking to your blog post and video. Try to enlist the promotional help of other (larger) blogs and Twitter accounts in your niche. More than likely, they'll be looking for compelling content to post, and this certainly fits the bill.

Once promotions are underway, you can begin slipping your tickets into your shipments, bags, books, and wherever else they belong. The tickets will sail off into the world.

Now it's your job to continue to promote the contest—trying to stir up a frenzy —while you wait for the winners to come forward. Watch Twitter closely for the winning messages.

When the winners appear, swing in and welcome them as though they were Twitter royalty. Write blog posts, craft emails, and send tweets in their honor. The spirit and immense effort behind this contest grant you the right to make a big to-do over the winners.

Once all the golden tickets are found—or at the end of the month, whichever comes first—ship out the prizes and thank everybody for playing. Also, this is probably a good time to take off your green top hat. People are looking at you funny.

Oompa.

CHAPTER 25

Real-World Scavenger Hunt

This is the most involved, time-intensive project in this book. Therefore, I've saved it for last. I can only recommend this project for established companies with a devout audience and a substantial prize to give away—like a car, vacation, or sizable cash prize. If you have the time and resources, and you want to make a splash in the world of social media, I challenge you to take on this project. And, if you do, I'd love to hear about it.

The basic idea of a scavenger hunt is simple. You lead people around a designated area using only clues you release to them on Twitter. When a participant reaches the final destination, he wins. The wonderful thing about scavenger hunts is how well they scale up and down. A scavenger hunt could be limited to the backyard at an 8-year-old's birthday party, or, as in the case of the Iron Butt Motorcycle Rally, it could span the continent and several days.

The scale of your scavenger hunt should make sense for your business and your audience. If you're attending a conference housed within a single hotel, you could lead your participants around the venue—from the meeting rooms to the buffet to the pool. If you own a chain of restaurants in Atlanta, it would be fun to lead your participants to all of your locations, maybe using the city's history for clues. If you own a national chain of outdoor outfitters (congratulations!), you could lead your participants to all the national parks in a month-long, well-advertised, well-documented race.

The first step in running a successful scavenger hunt is to pick interesting locations along the route that make sense when coupled with your business. Obviously, if your venue is limited, then your options for appropriate locations will be limited. "Over by the fern tree" may not make sense for your business, but it may make one heck of a great hiding spot.

Next, put together a list of compelling clues that will lead people to those various locations. Be sure to come up with more than one clue for each location in case you've accidentally thrown in a real stumper and no one figures out the original clue.

Put together a list of phrases for people to tweet out to prove they've reached a location. These phrases are a great promotional moment, so be creative! For example:

> "Running all over Atlanta to win my favorite burritos from Sal's Burrito Hut #myscavengerhunt"
> "This conference is the best ever. You should come! #conferencetag #myscavengerhunt"
> "Chicago to LA in 20 hours. I need some JOLT COLA! #myscavengerhunt"

Finally, you need to choose a prize. The prize will need to be substantial enough to make people want to jump all the hurdles you're placing in their way. (I recommend giving away something more creative—and more related to your audience—than just the latest product from Apple. Unless, of course, you're Apple. Hi, Apple.)

Write up a blog post, flyer, or booklet detailing the rules. They should go something like the following, but feel free to tweak where needed.

Rules:

- All participants must follow @myusername on Twitter to be eligible. All participants must also follow the clues in order, beginning with the first clue, which will be sent as a tweet out at the designated starting time to participants using the hashtag #myscavengerhunt.

- Once you arrive at each location, find the card within the (blue, red, white, etc.) envelope and tweet the saying written on that card out to your followers, along with the hashtag #myscavengerhunt.

- Once we receive the tweeted location phrase from you, we will send you a private direct message on Twitter with the clue for the next location.

- If you come to a location with a sealed envelope, you are the first to arrive at the last location. Open the envelope and read the question on the card. Take a photo of yourself in front of the last location and tweet the photo along with your answer to the question on the card. If you are the first to publicly tweet the correct answer to the question on the last card—along with your photo and the #myscavengerhunt hashtag—you will have won the (car, vacation, money, handshake, Carl's voice on your home answering machine, etc.)! Congratulations!

Once the scavenger hunt is over and you've given away all your prizes, use the winner's tweeted photo for some extra post-hunt write-ups about how much fun you had. Invite more audience members to play next time, and remind them about your weekly Twitter events—discussion groups, contests, giveaways, etc.

This project is fast-paced, incredibly fun, and makes a lot of positive noise about your company. But, as you can see, it also requires a lot of time, thought, and energy. Therefore, for most companies, it can't become a weekly occurrence. Try it out at your annual conference, at a trade show, a sales event, Black Friday, Arbor Day, or what-have-you. Happy hunting!

About the Author

Jesse McDougall has over 12 years of experience as a web designer, programmer, and web strategist. He speaks about web strategy and content marketing at conferences across the country and is the author of eight books about conducting business on the web. He is the co-owner of Catalyst Webworks, a web design and strategy firm focusing on the book publishing industry with clients across the US. He enjoys skiing, motorcycling, camping, motorcycle-camping, and ski-motorcycling. Currently, he lives in Vermont.

Have it your way.

Get even more for your money.

Join the O'Reilly Community, and register the O'Reilly books you own. It's free, and you'll get:

- $4.99 ebook upgrade offer
- 40% upgrade offer on O'Reilly print books
- Membership discounts on books and events
- Free lifetime updates to ebooks and videos
- Multiple ebook formats, DRM FREE
- Participation in the O'Reilly community
- Newsletters
- Account management
- 100% Satisfaction Guarantee

Signing up is easy:

1. **Go to: oreilly.com/go/register**
2. **Create an O'Reilly login.**
3. **Provide your address.**
4. **Register your books.**

Note: English-language books only

To order books online:

oreilly.com/store

For questions about products or an order:

orders@oreilly.com

To sign up to get topic-specific email announcements and/or news about upcoming books, conferences, special offers, and new technologies:

elists@oreilly.com

For technical questions about book content:

booktech@oreilly.com

To submit new book proposals to our editors:

proposals@oreilly.com

O'Reilly books are available in multiple DRM-free ebook formats. For more information:

oreilly.com/ebooks

O'REILLY®

Spreading the knowledge of innovators   oreilly.com

CPSIA information can be obtained at www.ICGtesting.com
Printed in the USA
LVOW122046240212

270299LV00016B/125/P